CONSEQUENCES

CONSEQUENCES

The making of a story-teller

by

Anne Melville

Old Pottery Press

First published in Great Britain in 1994
by The Old Pottery Press
Larkins Lane
Headington OX3 9DW

A catalogue record for this book
is available from the British Library

ISBN 0 9522472 0 8

Printed in Great Britain

CONTENTS

Preface

How one thing leads to another!

At the end of his first term at Oxford, in 1976, my son brought a fellow-undergraduate home for a visit: a well-mannered young woman who realised that it was her duty as a guest to make small-talk over lunch. She leaned forward over the table to address me.

'Tell me,' she asked earnestly, 'what is your philosophical position?'

A moment's hesitation and I should have been branded for ever as a moron or (much the same thing in the eyes of an eighteen-year-old) a housewife. I didn't hesitate even for a second.

'I'm a determinist,' I said.

The conversation continued. It must be born in mind that this was long before the beating of a butterfly's wings had wafted a garbled version of the chaos theory into the general consciousness, so I was in no position to appeal to science for support. Hannah, it appeared, had herself been a determinist for a short time in her youth, although by now she had seen the flaws in the theory. She explained these kindly, as someone who was one day to teach philosophy at Harvard, but I hardly bothered to listen. I was more interested in trying to decide whether my instinctive answer had been a truthful one.

As a general rule I dislike the use of labels to describe points of view -- probably because I have difficulty in remembering exactly what they stand for. It is likely that the meaning I give to the word determinist would not be accepted for a moment by a professional philosopher. So I apply my own definition, and it sums up an attitude to life with which I am content.

I was first introduced to the concept at the same age as my eighteen-year-old guest, and in the same university. It was in the hall of Magdalen College, with its smell of several centuries of boiled cabbage, that Gilbert Ryle gave a series of lectures on the many different approaches to antecedent truth which might be used to justify a general belief in predestination.

At the beginning of each lecture he blew his nose violently before considering whether the choice of not blowing his nose had ever existed. I scribbled the extensive notes for which women undergraduates in that era were renowned, and summed up the course more frivolously in bad verse.

Ryle blew his nose at twelve o'clock today
Because he had a cold, because it rained last night,
Because long ago a causal chain was started
And we cannot stop it, nor hope to set it right.

There were other verses for other theories, but I had already chosen the one which appealed to me. Every action has a consequence. Every event has a cause.

This theory is of dubious value to a novelist: it has certainly made me obsessed with the concept of reasonableness. Not for me the capricious heroine or the sudden soar into fantasy of a hero whose motives are incomprehensible. It's allowable that the characters in my books may fail to understand the motivation for their own actions, but vital that I, their creator, should always be able to answer the question 'Why?'

Such an attitude curtailed my career as a writer of children's books. Nine were published, each with a young central character who was sometimes unwise and often naughty but who always made the effort to be sensible. The tenth was returned with the comment that it was far too middle class. 'Kids these days want to read about characters who are zany.' A zany imagination, alas, is not one of my talents.

Books for adults are less easily narrowed by fashion and in that field I have continued to link cause and effect. Whether or not this emphasis makes a story too predictable for the reader I don't know, but for the writer it offers great intellectual pleasure. During the 1970s I wrote a series of six books about a single family, the Lorimers -- six hundred thousand words in all to chronicle the adventures of the different generations over a hundred years. The greatest satisfaction was to pick up in the fifth volume a trivial incident that had occurred in the first one, a century earlier, and reveal its literally life-shattering consequence -- in the knowledge that every step towards that moment had been faithfully, if unobtrusively, recorded in the intermediate books.

Similar satisfactions came in plotting the careers of minor characters. Kate Lorimer, the daughter of a British missionary, was born in Jamaica but found herself, as a young doctor, in Petrograd at the time of the October Revolution. Her presence there might seem surprising, even unlikely; but in fact her adventures over the previous years had carried her in that direction so inevitably that in the end there was nowhere else in the world she could reasonably have arrived. There is nothing to boast about in this. It is the proper definition of a plot. Something happens and something else occurs as a result. Not 'And then' but 'And therefore'.

Why should fictional characters alone be driven by the requirements of plot: the continuous process of cause and effect? The same progression is at work in real life. Something happens and something else occurs as a result. The only difference is that the connection in life is not always quite so clear.

Professor Ryle, I recall, in another of his lectures, discussed the theological argument for predestination.

> *Ryle blew his nose at twelve o'clock today.*
> *What God omniscient, creator, all strong*
> *Knew in his timelessness that this was bound to happen?*
> *So it had to be, or God himself would be proved wrong.*

As one of God's potential characters, I find this theory unattractive. As a kind of god in my own right, the sole creator of the characters in my books, I adopt it with pleasure. But even so it must remain subject to the higher rule. Every action has a consequence. Every event has a cause.

In life, as opposed to creative writing, these two statements offer an acceptable, even comfortable approach. Recognising the linkage of cause and effect has an effect of its own. For about two years, when I was sixteen and seventeen, I carried everywhere in my purse a small piece of paper, elaborately folded and becoming increasingly dirty as time passed.

The message on it, cunningly disguised in code, was brief. 'Somebody's got to: why not me?' (A confession now to an adolescent motto of such extreme ugliness, wrapped in such childish secrecy, may be taken as an indication of honesty to come.)

The subtlety of the message to my sixteen-year-old eyes was that it could encourage ambition ('Somebody's got to win') but could also make tolerable the acceptance of defeat ('Somebody's got to lose'). It was all part of an attitude to life which even then combined hopefulness when planning ahead with a certain stoicism as far as past events are concerned. Once disaster has struck and the last chance of avoiding it has disappeared, it must be accepted for what, with hindsight, it always was -- the inevitable result of a complicated pattern of historical threads. And yet there can be no sense of passivity in regard to the future; no requirement of acceptance in advance. It is always necessary to act as though our choices are unlimited. Only when one choice has been made can it be seen that no other was possible.

For some people that realisation is enough to make any decision at all seem unbearably difficult. 'Simply to choose stopped up all ways but one,' wrote Philip Larkin to the wife he never had. I approach from the opposite side, seeing any decision, once made, as being so inevitable that there is no point in wasting time on wonderings or regrets. It has made for contentment, although perhaps for a lack of adventure.

In my work as a novelist I look forward, plotting crises and their consequences for my characters. Away from my desk, if I consider my own life, it is equally fascinating to look back, extracting from a confusion of activity the relevant cause of a particular effect. It seems to me, as I consider this, that everything of any importance in adulthood has grown from seeds of experience sown before my eighteenth birthday.

No doubt this is true of everyone.

A hole in the head

1

How odd it was that nobody would let me go to sleep! In the spring of 1931, when I was five and three-quarters, my usual daily timetable ended with a six o'clock bedtime. By that hour my mother should have read me a story, tucked me in and kissed me goodnight. As a rule I was the one who fought against this rigid ending of the day -- or else, acquiring subtlety, waited until the door was closed before creeping out of bed to find my book and read it by the light of the evening sun or the street lamp outside the window.

On this particular evening, however, our roles had been reversed. I longed for sleep, continually attempting to slide down under the sheets whilst my parents, taking it in turns, pulled me up again to sit propped up by pillows and forced to keep awake. My father read to me, story after story. My mother tried to persuade me to recite with her some of the poems we had learned together or made shadow pictures on the wall with her fingers. I can still recall the shape of the little baggy-trousered Dutch boy. 'Let's call him Jan,' she said. 'Shall we make up some adventures for him?' I don't imagine that I answered. I can only remember the heavy desire for sleep.

This is not the earliest memory of my life, which in its first five years contained the usual small dramas of most little girls. I have no recollection of the house in which I was born, in a poor area of Harrow. But by the time I was three my parents, although frightening themselves by the size of their mortgage, had taken a double step up the housing ladder and moved into a five-bedroomed semi-detached house.

My own contribution to the move was the delightful task of bursting the blisters of old paint and then trying to rub them flat. I had a garden now in which to play -- and my mother's relentless photography began. The results were cut out and pasted into albums with twee captions. 'First little friend' was a kitten. 'Ahoy there!' featured a toy boat in a tin bath. One of the photographs shows me rubbing down the paintwork. So do I really remember the act itself, or only the record of it? It's too late now to be sure.

It was not long after the move that I was packed off to live with friends of my mother's for what seemed an eternity but was perhaps only three or four weeks. No explanation was given to ease my bewilderment;

and only many years later did I discover that this was the period in which the only baby brother I was ever to have was born and died.

More exciting was the first day at Greenhill Elementary School. Miss James, the club-footed ruler of the Beginner's Class, led me to a table. I was to stick coloured paper on to a card in the shape of a yacht. One of my fellow-beginners was so terrified by the whole operation that she wet her knickers in the middle of the classroom floor under the wide-eyed gaze of all the other five-year-olds, but I had the confidence which came from already being a fluent reader. My mother had been a primary school teacher before her marriage and had led me rapidly through a reading course entitled Songs the Letters Sing.

All these events were interesting, but lacked the significance of the evening which was to prove the start of a nightmare. For my parents the nightmare had begun much earlier. In those days before antibiotics, mastoiditis could be a killer. No wonder I was not allowed to sleep that night, in case I should never awaken.

I must suppose that I had been ill for some time before that heavy drowsiness descended. My earlier screams of pain have been described to me, but I have no memory of them at all -- a curious contrast with my ability to relive the discomfort which came later. I was being kept awake that evening until the arrival of an ambulance. Neither then nor later did my parents either own or drive a car.

The ambulance rattled from Harrow, a suburb of London, into the middle of the city: to the Royal Ear, Nose and Throat Hospital. Before that day I had travelled on buses, but always, of course, sitting up. Now, lying on a stretcher, I felt the vibrations as a violent shuddering, as though all the streets were cobbled. I wondered where we were going.

The ambulance drew to a halt and I was transferred to a trolley which was pushed very fast through a long tunnel covered in tiles. The vibrations beneath were of a different kind now, rattling with a frightening urgency. When I managed to raise my head I could see my parents hurrying behind. They had difficulty in keeping up and, although they walked fast, from time to time they had to take a few steps at a run. When the tunnel came to an end and the trolley was pushed inside a room, they were, I think, left outside. It was to be some time before I was conscious of seeing them again.

Inside the room, still flat on my back, I stared up at a very bright light. The room began to fill with people: seven or eight men who must have been medical students -- but I did not yet know that I was in a hospital. One of the men, who was not a student but a surgeon, took out a torch in the shape of a long and very fat pencil and pressed the point of it hard into my ear.

I was the beloved only child of kind parents. No one had ever inflicted pain on me like the agony caused by that pressure. I hated the man who did it with the full-blooded rage which perhaps can only be experienced by a child to whom no explanations have been given.

Like any normal adult I have since that day had quarrels which filled me with a temporary fury. There are people whom I never want to see again. There are a few who have filled me with a revulsion for which I can find no good reason, and others for whom I feel a coldness which can be disguised only by polite and businesslike behaviour. But I am certainly not quarrelsome and would not describe myself as unforgiving. So it was a strange moment when, very many years after that first encounter, I read the name of the surgeon in the obituary column of The Times and felt again the surge of a hatred which had never died.

As an older child I found excuses for my anger. When the first operation had to be followed by others over a period of several years, I told myself that if the surgeon had done it properly the first time, there would have been no need for repeats: that is the way that a ten-year-old may be expected to argue. At first I blamed him for not cutting away enough of the bone to start with. Later I found myself with a hole behind the ear which to this day has never healed but remains open to infection or to irritation from the chemicals in shampoos or swimming pools and makes it inadvisable for me to dive or swim under water in case I black out. Naturally I grumbled then that he had cut away too much.

Another reason for anger dawned on me only slowly. It was in those days -- the 1930s -- the boast of leading surgeons and physicians that they operated a Robin Hood system which made any kind of state welfare scheme unnecessary. They charged high fees to their rich patients in order that they could afford to care at low cost for their poor ones.

We might have hoped to be beneficiaries of this policy. My father, a junior civil servant in the executive grade, had a salary which was secure but small. With unfortunate timing, however, he had just begun a secondary career as Bernard Newman, author and lecturer: the career which much later was to provide his whole livelihood. A recently-published book had met with considerable acclaim. Newspapers were generous then in their allocation of space for book reviews, and the scrapbooks into which he pasted his first cuttings contain more column inches than my own first twenty books together would accumulate.

The surgeon, I suppose, read the reviews and concluded that my father was a rich man. He could not have known that the publisher of the book had gone bankrupt before paying any royalties. When the medical bills started to come in, my father almost went bankrupt himself. He was a shy man who perhaps did not realise that it might have been possible to negotiate. I was an expensive child for him, and the experience left him nervous about money for the rest of his life. When my mother, much later, became an invalid, his anxiety lest she should one day be left a widow without the means to pay any necessary nursing fees made him reluctant to spend money on anything at all. I was to suffer considerably from this attitude when I became an undergraduate -- but since I was the cause of it in the first place, perhaps this was only fair.

The more immediate effect on myself, as soon as I was old enough to comprehend what had happened, was a very early understanding of the anxiety, up to the point of disaster, which could be brought on a poor or even middle-income family by a medical emergency. I became a fervent supporter of a national health service long before any such thing existed: it must have provided my first thread of political awareness.

All that lay in the future. For the moment I lay still, hurt and frightened and abandoned, while each medical student in turn peered through the torch into my ear. Then there is a gap in memory. But it was not, I think, very much later that I was lying on another high bed beneath another bright light. My arms were strapped down. A mask was pressed over my face and suddenly I was unable to breathe. Trying to struggle free, I found myself a prisoner. I held my breath, closing my lungs to the gas with which, it seemed, someone was trying to kill me -- but knowing that sooner or later I would have to succumb.

Twenty years later, told that an operation would be needed to deal with an impacted wisdom tooth, I refused pointblank to have a general anaesthetic, preferring to endure any pain rather than experience again that feeling of suffocation. The nurse looked at me curiously. 'It's only a little prick of a needle,' she said. 'You'll hardly feel it, and you'll be asleep before you know what's happening.' I was still a young woman then; but the days of the chloroform pad and the ether mask had already, it seemed, passed into history: the antediluvian practice of an earlier generation.

It was a moment which left its mark on a five-year-old. The pressing down of the mask gave me my first experience of terror -- and the last. As though it provided a kind of immunisation, nothing in the future was ever to induce the same feeling of panic again. But at the time it was horrifying enough. As I sank helplessly into darkness, a tall, thin man came to stand over me, staring down while he waited for my eyes to close. He wore a mask now, but I recognised him as the man who had earlier hurt my ear. I suppose that almost certainly Mr Scott-Stevenson saved my life that night, but I never forgave him. There is no logic to ingratitude.

2

After the operation came a long stay in the children's ward of the hospital. It was here that I heard for the first time the question which was still being put by one child to another when I worked as a voluntary playlady in the Great Ormond Street Hospital for Sick Children forty years later.

'Are you medical or surgical?'

'What's the difference?'

'Medical's when you're ill before you come in. Surgical's when they make you ill after you get here.'

I was surgical, and inevitably my first weeks in the ward were painful. The hole in my head was packed with a dressing: a very long thin strip which was pressed in a little at a time. The insertion of the dressing felt like a series of hammer blows, to be endured in misery. Its extraction was almost equally painful, but with a curiously different effect. It was always the prelude to another packing-in, so there was no prospect of relief as the long strip was gradually tugged out. But it was a sharp pain instead of a dull one and -- like the wiggling of a first tooth which is not quite ready to fall out -- it seemed possible to enjoy it even while complaining that it hurt.

Not to be described as pain was the headache which persisted for many weeks. By day it was a dull throbbing. At night it expressed itself more dramatically, in the form of nightmare. I suppose now that nightmare is a frequent -- perhaps even an inevitable -- consequence of head injury, even when the injury is inflicted by a surgeon. At the time, of course, it appeared to be an experience unique to myself; and I am not yet prepared to discard the belief, held for many years, that my career as a story-teller began at the age of five, when I did battle with my nightmares and beat them.

They were always torture situations. Slow torture: dreams not of extreme pain but of something creeping and inexorable. I was inside a closed room, lacking doors or windows, which gradually filled with water or sand. For a little while I could keep my head above it, but gradually I would be pressed up against the ceiling. On the first few occasions I woke up screaming, and had to be soothed back to sleep by the night nurse. But gradually I acquired the art of taking the plot, so to speak, into my own hands and transforming a sleeping nightmare into a waking, if drowsy, daydream. It became possible to stop the flow of water, the trickle of sand. I was still inside the room, but nothing worse could happen.

That was only the start of the manipulation. The realisation grew that by embarking on the daydream and working it through before I fell asleep, before the nightmare had a chance to start, I could make the whole story run to my own specification. Suddenly I was not inside the room but outside, looking in through walls and ceilings made of glass. The slow torture continued, but now I had become the torturer and not the victim.

I began consciously to invent new predicaments for the shadowy figure who was suffering and who was not myself; and gloated over my control. The other children in the ward provided storylines which would otherwise have been outside my very limited experience. One had impaled himself on the spike of a railing: one had sucked a rusty nail through a cotton reel with such energy that it pierced his throat. Both these actual boys died behind drawn curtains in the bed next to mine; but in my invented stories I could use their tragedies as a threat which I had the power to avert as well as to inflict. I began to look forward to the moment when the lights were dimmed so that I could begin a new story in my head or take one up where I had left it the previous evening.

Although I don't think that I can have been taken to the cinema before the age of five, I ran my stories as films, seeing them as moving pictures and not as patterns of words. Daydreaming led me peacefully to sleep, and the sleep was no longer shattered by screams.

Ten years later I was still sending myself to sleep with daydreams. By then -- of course! -- their subjects were romantic encounters with some worshipped film star, or the search for the fascinating 'real' parents who must surely have given me away to be brought up by the couple I called Mummy and Daddy. When, as an adolescent, I remembered the pleasure I had taken in cruelty in those early plots, I was filled with guilt, horrified by what I saw as an innate sadism. That guilt has long disappeared. The wound in my head was as much responsible for the content of the daydreams as it was for the nightmares.

The consequence of that early habit has been lifelong. I still lie awake, creating characters and making up adventures for them to enjoy or endure: the only difference is that now in the darkness I think in words, waiting until I am sitting at my desk before the scenes are allowed to flow like a film. There have been times when I have had trouble in completing a novel, but I can't remember that there has ever been an occasion when I was unable to start. Putting words on to paper has, over the years, become almost an obsession. To be deprived of the power to continue, for whatever reason, would be a recipe for unhappiness. Making up stories in my head is a habit which goes even deeper. When I can no longer do it, I shall be dead.

Perhaps I should have developed the habit even without the help of the mastoid operation. My father, after all, was a story-teller before me. Whether or not such an aptitude can be genetically transmitted, there must certainly be an effect on any child of seeing in practice a way of life which results in a particular achievement.

My father thought up his plots while walking or cycling. He liked to have company, and I was his favourite; but the company had to keep quiet. From a very young age I understood that if somebody went for a long walk in complete silence, sooner or later a book would arrive with his name printed on it -- and over the years an increasing number of books written by Bernard Newman appeared on our bookshelves. I don't recall that as a small child I ever consciously resolved to be a writer myself. But when eventually one of my stories seemed to demand to be set down on paper, family background made writing appear to be a normal activity.

So no doubt both heredity and environment go some way to explain the fact that at the moment of writing this I have almost fifty published books on my own shelves (a meagre number compared with my father's hundred and forty) as well as boxes full of unpublished manuscripts. But so many writers are revealed by their biographies to have suffered some kind of prolonged childhood illness that there must surely be a strong causal link here. Although my father's example may have encouraged me to start writing, first of all there has to be an urge to create and the habit of organising a plot. There has never been any doubt in my mind about where I acquired that habit. When I was five and three-quarters a surgeon made a hole in my head. The consequence was, I became a novelist.

3

The memory of the operation receded. My head was still ill, but the rest of my body was healthy, demanding exercise. Other children were admitted to the ward. Some died and some recovered: their beds were taken by other young patients. I seemed to be the only one who was not allowed to go home. Why not?

After a time my need for movement was recognised. I was allowed out of bed and dressed in day clothes -- not my own -- from a box kept for this purpose. The centre of the long ward was a good place for playing: for rolling wheeled toys or pedalling a small tricycle up and down. And I could chatter to the other children who were still confined to bed. I can't imagine that any of this boisterous activity on my part did much for their recovery. But if I was allowed to play in the ward, why couldn't I go and play at home?

The reason given in answer to my frequent requests was the daily need to change my dressing. I believed it, but it wasn't true. It had already been decided that I needed another operation, to remove tonsils and adenoids. No doubt it was my frantic reaction to the earlier anaesthetic which made it necessary to conceal this prospect from me. Although it seems hard to believe, I must have spent a minimum of three months in the ward, waiting until I was strong enough to survive more surgery. This long wait was to have two consequences. One was trivial: the other was sad.

The trivial consequence was that I became fat. Perhaps this would have happened in any case, for both my parents were large. But all those early photographs in the garden of 3 Gerard Road show a little girl of normal size.

In the hospital, however, it appeared that a deliberate decision had been taken to fatten me up. The medium chosen was milk. There was milk to drink and porridge to eat for breakfast; a hot milk drink at eleven, rice pudding at lunch time, more milk for tea and Horlicks or Ovaltine at the end of the day.

Even at the time I realised that something very close to forced feeding was taking place, and objected strongly but without success. Before my illness I had drunk milk as a matter of course. By the time I left hospital I loathed the taste of it and if someone today tried to make me drink a glass I would be sick before I started. If either of my children should ever doubt that they were 'wanted' babies I would point to the self-sacrifice with which

I forced myself during pregnancy to swallow the huge amounts of this disgusting liquid declared to be necessary for the future health of their bones and teeth.

Presumably this regime had the desired effect of building up my strength; but when combined with the inevitable lack of exercise it sent me -- eventually -- back into the outside world as a roly-poly. The fact that there were still three more years of recurrent illness to come did not prove helpful. I was podgy as a child, 'sturdy' as a young woman, fat in middle age and, if this is a time for straight talking, obese as I grew older.

I was also, when I emerged from hospital at the age of six, weak on my legs. Whether or not all that milk had fortified my constitution, it had done nothing for my muscles. My mother's solution was to enrol me at a children's dancing class. Since I could hardly walk, much less hop or jump, this was not a success. Humiliated, I began to believe that I was not and never would be any good at physical activity. This quite unnecessary impression was to lead to years of running battles with gym mistresses who rightly accused me of not trying as I made feeble attempts to vault over horses.

It did not, however, inspire me with any urge to change my shape. In those early years I would have had no hope, since the feeding-up process was continued by my anxious mother after I returned home, and any attempt to leave part of an over-generous helping on the plate prompted the exhortation that I must think of the starving miners. Later, when adolescent anxiety might have been expected to take control, there proved to be two good reasons why I should accept my body as it was.

The first of these was the example of my mother. In middle age she was a stout woman, and ashamed of it. Rigidly corseted with whalebone and laces, she made effort after effort to reduce her size.

There was the grapefruit period, the Epsom salts period, the liquid-only period and the no-liquid period. There was a period when the bathroom became almost impossible to enter after the erection of a wooden structure which served as a kind of Turkish bath. And -- most dangerous of all --- there was a long period in which she bought weekly bottles of thyroid tablets which she ate like sweets.

Whether or not there is any medical justification for this view, I assumed when she eventually took to her bed that such over-indulgence must have been a contributory cause of the angina from which she was to suffer for the last twenty years of her life. I had no wish to emulate my mother's obsession with her size and weight and have always found dieting to be the most boring of all conversational subjects. No doubt it would have been sensible to look for a middle way, but instead I made an early decision not to worry about my weight but to save my mental energy for more important matters. There have been moments when I have sighed over some article of clothing which is suitable only for some fashionable stick-person, but in general a lack of elegance has seemed a small price to pay for a lack of body-anxiety.

It might have changed my attitude if I had felt myself to be unhealthy; but by the time I was fourteen I discovered with surprise that I was not a no-hoper in the physical sphere at all and instead rated quite high for stamina. Perhaps all those silent cycle rides with my father had had their effect. I could walk almost indefinitely, skate with speed although not with grace, climb any of the modest mountains to be found in Great Britain and explore the countryside on a bicycle with rides of up to ninety miles a day. It should be remembered that this was before the era of mountain bikes, and even a three-speed gear was beyond my pocket: ninety miles was an ambitious distance.

Another moment of doubt might well have come when -- in the 'sturdy' stage -- I first fell in love with Jeremy, my future husband. But he -- claiming to prefer Rubens to Modigliani -- was prepared to love me as I was: and, indeed, quoted with affectionate memory a Mabel Lucie Attwell picture from his childhood. The illustration can easily be imagined. The text ran: 'What if I am fat; I have a happy disposition.' Quite.

Now that I have passed sixty, my GP plots my weight and height on a chart every three years and tuts as he points out the orange square on which I stand, dangerously near to the red. Almost hopefully he enquires whether I suffer from backache or breathlessness. I am tempted to answer by challenging him to a game of tennis, which I still play at least once a week in all seasons, long after many of my slimmer contemporaries have reduced their exercise to the gentle dead-heading of roses.

It may well be that one of the consequences of my childhood illness was later obesity but, if so, it's of no importance. There was another consequence which was to matter a great deal more.

4

The idea that young children in hospital needed to have their parents at hand was still almost unheard-of in 1931. Visiting hours in the children's ward were in the afternoon. It must have been a kind-hearted matron who realised that my father could never leave work at this time and allowed him to call in each morning on his way to the office. He couldn't stay long -- just long enough to present me with the daily offering of a thin penny bar of Nestlé's chocolate, wrapped in scarlet paper with a picture tucked inside to be collected; but I looked forward to his visits and loved him for them.

My mother was different. Perhaps she did in fact visit me at the beginning of my stay, but if so a later resentment on my part drove all memory of this from my mind. Certainly long before the end of it she had ceased to come at all. Visiting time, when most of the other children had someone sitting at the bedside, was the most miserable period of the day for me. In the interests of peace and quiet I was not allowed to play on the floor, but had to stay in bed, and soon ceased to watch the door hopefully. Instead, as the bell rang for visitors to be admitted, I kept my eyes firmly on my book, prepared to be sulky rather than appreciative if this should prove to be the only day when someone would come to sit beside me.

Time passed and I was judged to be strong enough for the operation to remove my tonsils and adenoids. Instead of having a mask forced over my face, I was offered a very special balloon to blow up: the feeling of suffocation was the same.

The nightmares began again, with a new ingredient: blood. I emerged from unconsciousness to find blood streaming from my mouth into an enamel bowl and it took a long time to forget that moment. Meanwhile there was a different area of discomfort, a further period of recuperation. But at last it was all over and I could go home.

My father came to fetch me. I was to have a new bedroom, he told me, larger than my old one. All my toys had been moved into it already and were waiting for me.

My mother was waiting as well, and had prepared a welcome tea worthy of a birthday party. I was allowed to look at it: laid out on the table were jam tarts, little iced cakes, chocolate finger biscuits and a jelly in two colours. Before I sat down, though, I must have my medicine. The doctors had insisted on regular doses, and if I took the first spoonful now, the lovely tea would soon take the taste away. And while I was enjoying the feast, they would have some exciting news to tell me. Just one spoonful, now.

The medicine was Parish's (or was it Parrish's?) Iron Tonic. It hit my throat, still sore from the tonsillectomy, like a paint stripper. There was never any chance that a mere chocolate biscuit would overwhelm that metallic taste. I gave a roar of indignation, turned my back on the tea table and ran upstairs to my bedroom for comfort.

I had forgotten that I was to sleep in a different room from now on, and it was the door of my old bedroom which I flung open. Understandably startled, the baby lying there in her cot began to cry.

I had been an only child for six years, and no doubt the arrival of a new baby would have been a difficult pill to swallow at the best of times. This was the worst of times. I had been left to suffer pain and loneliness in hospital because my mother had a new little girl to love. Everything that I had been unable to understand at the time suddenly seemed to became clear to me. In the years which followed I was never able to feel any great affection for my sister Hilary; and I never loved my mother again.

Although she seemed to me to have done everything wrong, she had been dealt a difficult hand to play. She had already suffered the loss of a greatly-desired son and was pregnant again when faced with the distress of my own emergency. Even in normal circumstances she was an over-emotional woman and it was not surprising if her doctor advised her to stay calmly at home for the sake of the new baby. Several years later, desperate to break through my lack of affection and knowing that I was more easily influenced by books than by feelings, she gave me a book on child psychology to read. She hoped that once I understood what had happened I would be able to forget it. But it was too late. I had already learned the lesson that love cannot be reasoned into existence.

The immediate result of my confrontation with Hilary was that I found my new bedroom and at once put myself myself to bed. My mother cried and the baby cried but I lay with my face to the wall, eyes screwed tightly shut in a pretence of sleep and throat still smarting from the tonic. I never did get to eat the welcome tea.

The consequence for my mother was a tragic one. For the first years of my life she had adored me and I had adored her in return. Now, suddenly, a curtain had come down between us, and it was never to rise again. There were no great scenes. On one or two later occasions I was heartless in doing what I wanted to without considering the possible effects on her; but I had been brought up to be good-mannered and to outward appearances I behaved well as a rule towards her, acting the part of the dutiful daughter. When I became a mother myself, I took the children regularly for her to enjoy. But it was never enough, and I knew it.

My father was not a demonstrative man. I was always confident of his love, but can never remember him kissing me at all, although twice in my life -- once on my wedding day and once on his deathbed -- I took the initiative in kissing him. My mother, by contrast, needed frequent physical displays of affection and had to rely on her daughters to provide these. It must have been humiliating for her to ask me -- as she frequently did -- to kiss her, knowing that I would do it only because I was asked.

The failure of this vital relationship in my own life had more complicated consequences. It fostered a high degree of emotional independence in me from an unusually early age: I have never suffered from loneliness. It also impelled me towards the decision that I never wanted to have children of my own, because I had learned from experience that children do not always like their mothers.

This decision, sincerely and strongly held, was to prove inconvenient when, at the age of twenty, I received a proposal of marriage that I longed to accept. Jeremy wanted children and I wanted Jeremy. The positive outweighed the negative and, after long discussion and with some anxiety on my part, I agreed that yes, we would have a family.

The unusual formality of this agreement, which no doubt most young couples take for granted, cast a shadow over several years of my early married life, for it soon became apparent that nature did not intend me to be a mother. Had some deficiency in my body unconsciously influenced that youthful decision not to have children, I had to ask myself, or was a lingering effect of that decision, now abandoned, causing my body to abort every pregnancy? After one stillbirth and five miscarriages, two of them painfully late, I might well have been tempted to give up. I had tried, after all. But I had made a promise and I was going to keep it. If mind and matter were doing battle, mind was going to win.

It was a relief, all the same, after months of tedious and sometimes painful treatment, to discover that it was the body and not the mind which was providing the stumbling block. A series of hormone implants enabled me to carry first one and then a second pregnancy to full term.

None of my fears have been realised. Jeremy was right -- as he usually is -- when he persuaded me in 1947 that our children would be delightful. As a family of four we like each other in a way which is even more satisfactory than the loving which lies behind it.

Jocelyn and Jonathan may perhaps have suffered when they were young from my eagerness to propel them into independence. I think my daughter was surprised, when she made the decision not to have children herself, that I was neither disappointed nor disapproving; and my son was certainly shocked when he first heard me expound the view that parenthood -- the inflicting of life (and therefore death) on someone who need never have existed -- is a wholly selfish activity.

Both those reactions on my part can be easily traced back to my own childhood; but the line of cause and effect takes a far more twisted course when required to explain the very existence of my daughter and son. I gave birth -- eventually -- to two children, whom I love, because I was unable to love my own mother.

Unwillingly to school

Now that I had left hospital at last it was time to return to school. This was not a straightforward process. After so much missed time there must have been doubts about whether I could keep up if I were to rejoin my original group. They, like myself, were all six years old now and no longer Beginners, for a new academic year had started. It was decided that I should be tested to see whether I would do better to start again from the bottom.

The test was simply to read aloud. I can remember standing in front of the headmaster -- a terrifying figure, for to his pupils his only known function was to administer punishments. I was handed three books in turn: presumably of different standards of difficulty. Thanks to my mother I had learned to read very young and during my long stay in hospital books had provided my chief recreation and comfort. My reading age was years ahead of my actual age. Instead of being demoted to repeat the Beginners' year, I was promoted to join an older group. This was not a success.

Reading was fine. Arithmetic was not too bad, because my mother was able to coach me to catch up and I could soon recite all my tables with the rest of the class. Writing was more of a problem, because I had missed out the stage of being taught how to use the graceful copperplate loops to join letters into words. Handwriting, legible handwriting, remains a problem to this day. As for drill and handwork, I was completely out of my depth. I can't remember how long I was left to struggle before being moved back amongst my contemporaries; but it was long enough to make me miserable.

There was plenty to be miserable about. Greenhill Elementary School was a grim building; built in the nineteenth century and without any blade of grass to soften its surroundings: the single tree whose roots were inside the playground leaned out over the brick wall as though it were as anxious as myself to escape. In the 1930s the building was lit by gas and heated, for the comfort of the teachers, by coal fires. The naughty boys who were summoned to sit in the front row of desks were no doubt warm enough: the good little girls at the back were left to shiver.

The school was situated in one of the poorer districts of Harrow -- the district from which my parents had moved as soon as they were able -- and the word which best described most of its pupils was 'rough'. They were aged from five to fourteen and during the morning and afternoon breaks the asphalt playground was ruled by the older boys, who played football in all seasons. Any small girl who wanted to skip or whip her top or play hop-scotch, according to the time of year, was liable to be sent flying by a ball or player. The only way to be safe was to sit on top of a pile of coal. I was not physically robust at this time and found the playground a threatening place.

It didn't help, of course, that my long absence and subsequent movement between classes had left me short of friends. And before long I had to face another problem. Just over a year after my return from hospital it was decided that a second operation was needed on my head. This time it took place in Harrow and my parents had learned their lesson. I was regularly visited and on Guy Fawkes Night my father brought fireworks to let off outside the window of the ward. And when I returned home my mother refused to undertake the daily change of the dressing in the wound, on the reasonable grounds that I had come to associate her with pain.

So a decision was made that I should call at the doctor's surgery on my way to school each day. The surgery opened at nine: the school gate closed at nine. The doctor's patients grumbled because I had a regular arrangement to jump the queue and be seen first; and the school monitor on duty took pleasure in closing the gate on me while he wrote my name in the penalty book, disregarding my plea that I had been given special permission to arrive late. In those days, when roads were safe to cross, it was taken for granted that children should go to school on their own; but for a seven-year-old this was a stressful start to the school day.

Another cause of stress would be waiting for me inside the building: my old enemy, milk. A crate of neat little bottles, each holding a third of a pint, was delivered to each classroom, and to drink the ration was compulsory. Sometimes the teacher would not be watching as a hardly-touched bottle was returned, and quite frequently a classmate would be glad to drink a double helping; but all too often I had to struggle to the bottom myself. There were few things nastier, I thought unhappily, than milk which has first of all frozen and then thawed to tepidity in front of a fire. Ugh!

To my general dislike of the school was added an element of snobbishness -- because of course Greenhill Elementary was not the only educational establishment on offer. Their ambitious house move had carried my parents into a street where everyone else was more prosperous than we were. Past our front door every morning walked boys striped like wasps in black and yellow blazers, and girls in the cerise uniform of Heathfield Girls' School: paying pupils. How I longed to go to Heathfield! There would be no rough boys -- indeed, no boys at all. I would come home clean and tidy, instead of covered with coal dust, and I would make congenial friends instead of being as much an outsider in the street as in school.

I don't recollect that my parents ever answered my pleas in so many words by saying that they couldn't afford to pay school fees; although no doubt that would have been true. What I do remember is their argument that 'ordinary' schools, like Greenhill, gave a better education: and I remember it because even before the age of eleven I suspected that was not true. My experience there made me determined later on, when I had children of my own, that they should go to the best schools we could find for them, of whatever kind.

Perhaps one only remembers the worst moments of schooldays, but I certainly have a good store of those, with no high spots to balance them. As I grew older I became less timorous in the playground, but still found unnerving the ritual caning ceremonies set up by the staff -- even though as a well-behaved pupil I was never likely to suffer that punishment myself.

Except for limping Miss James of the Beginners and mousy Miss Billings in what was hopefully called the Scholarship Class, the teachers were bullies. I remember in particular a mountainously huge man, too lazy to move, called (can this be right?) Mr Mahogany, who summoned pupils to stand by his desk so that he could pull their ears.

Most lessons were taken by the form teacher, allowing little escape from an unkind one; but art was taught in all the upper forms by Mr Shaw. At home I took pleasure in painting 'designs', making intricate patterns with ruler and compass, sometimes on paper and sometimes to decorate the wooden egg cups or matchbox holders or pencil boxes which could be bought 'naked' and later given as Christmas presents. But this was not Art.

Mr Shaw's art was done at ordinary school desks with fixed seats, so that it was not easy, for example, to slope a water colour at exactly the right angle for a graduated colour wash to ooze gently down the paper. Over and over again my knuckles were painfully rapped with a brass-trimmed ruler, convincing me that I would never be any good at painting. Many years later, in adult education classes, I discovered that painting was a pleasure and sculpture sheer delight. Only then did I realise that I had genuine cause for resentment against the man who had spoilt it for me for twenty years.

I was still at this school when it was decided that a third operation on my head was necessary. Although it seems unlikely, I have such a clear memory of the day that I can say for certain that it took place in my own house. Perhaps it was an extreme emergency -- or perhaps, on the other hand, it was less serious than the earlier ones and did not necessitate the trauma of a return to hospital. I came home from a visit to a friend of my mother's to find the house smelling of ether and disinfectant: the first sniff was enough to alarm me. I ran upstairs: all the bedclothes had been removed from my bed. It and everything else in the room had been covered with white sheets. Somewhere in the house, I had no doubt, was the hated surgeon. Determined to resist, I can remember dashing into my parents' bedroom for protection. Lying pale and unmoving in that room was my three-year-old sister Hilary. I was so sure that she must be dead that I checked my attempt to hide and was quickly caught and undressed. She was in fact seriously ill with bronchitis: yet again my unfortunate mother had been forced to cope with two sick children at once.

From this operation I emerged with a bandaged head, and on the evidence of photographs the bandage remained in place for many months. (The consequence of this is that either it flattened one of two sticking-out ears or else it forced one of my neatly flat ears to stick out: I shall never know which.)

The bandage earned me a measure of relief from the rough and tumble of the school playground. There may have been some feeling that I might break if knocked over too violently. In any case, I had by now ceased to be nervous and had become both a tomboy and a guttersnipe, as untidy and dirty as all the other pupils.

The gutters were literally of interest, since they contained not only conkers in season but discarded cigarette packets -- and I was an avid collector of cigarette cards. Eagerly I pulled the silver paper away from the cardboard in the hope that it would reveal something more interesting than yet another cricketer or military uniform of the British Empire. I encouraged my mother to smoke as much as possible, buying her favourite Craven A in packets of five rather than in twenties whenever I was sent to do the shopping. At home I filled albums: at school I flicked and swapped. Indirectly I absorbed a certain amount of information from the text on the back of each card and still think with affection of Wills' Household Hints whenever I tackle a difficult stain or prepare a pot plant to survive a holiday.

Gutters were also ideal for playing games of marbles on the move. By the age of nine or ten I had acquired a talent for this particular playground game and could do so many things with marbles that boys were sometimes prepared to play with me instead of knocking me over. New games were invented with elaborate rules and much use of chalk. I had a good eye, and my winnings grew. The swirls of colour inside each glass ball delighted me and when not engaged in play I would gloat over my collection, sorting them into colours as a card player might sort suits. Each colour had its own character. I especially valued the staunchness of butterscotch, whereas yellow was feeble and could be lost in a gamble without anxiety. Most beautiful of all, of course, were the large alleys and taws, some of them as beautifully patterned with delicate spirals of colour as the most precious Venetian glass. It took a strong nerve to put one of these at risk as a stake.

Although my passion for playing marbles probably lasted for only two or three seasons, it helped to inspire the writing of *Lochandar* and had a direct consequence in providing me with a hobby to fill a later period of my life. In my mid-fifties Jeremy and I spent a few days with friends in South Africa. The family had its own bowling green and a regular weekly game. We were invited to join in, and separated so that each team should only be burdened with one beginner. As soon as I felt the bowl in my hand I remembered the pleasure I had once taken in propelling little balls along the ground and knew that I was about to enjoy myself.

The principle of the bias was explained and we were allowed a trial end or two to practise delivering our borrowed bowls in the curve which would bring them gently back to rest against the jack. I realised that by increasing the speed of the bowl I could reduce its curve and with my last practice turn produced what I later discovered to be called a firing shot, straight down the middle to hit the jack off the green. To the one-time under-eleven marbles champion of Greenhill Elementary, there was nothing to it. It had to be explained to me kindly that this was not precisely the object of the game and that any firing needed would be done by the skip, or captain, of the team. So when the game proper started I behaved as a beginner should, following the curve which was pointed out for me and enjoying a considerable amount of beginner's luck. I enjoyed the controlled movement of delivery and quickly came to appreciate the subtle approaches made possible by the bias and the intellectual challenge of plotting a position and creating it.

In short, I was hooked. Soon after returning home to London I enrolled myself at Paddington Indoor Bowling Club, not caring that I didn't know a single member of it. I must have been a considerable puzzle when I first arrived, for most of the large membership was male and the small number of women who played there had all been introduced to the game by their husbands. So who was this lone female who turned up to practise by herself? I had had no coaching other than on that first afternoon in South Africa; and to start with I wore the wrong clothes, because the helpful shop which sold me bowls and bowling shoes omitted to mention that I would need to wear uniform: white blouse and grey skirt. None of this worried me. Unlike a tennis player or cricketer, a bowler can perfectly well play by herself if she chooses, inventing rules and targets for a solitary game just as a child can do with marbles.

In retirement -- Jeremy's, not mine -- we moved within reach of a club at which I could bowl both indoors and out of doors and I found myself becoming competitive. Although not a county player I have had enough good days at ordinary club level to bring a succession of silver cups through the house: nowadays, alas, they are never presented for keeps. My husband and son are both successful games players and I find it amusing that I should have joined them so late in life. Amusing, but not necessarily surprising. It may have taken me a long time to make the progression, but the seed of my present enthusiasm for bowls was certainly sown on the asphalt playground of Greenhill Elementary School.

Greenhill kept its pupils until they were fourteen before tipping them out into the labour market, but there was one escape hatch. This was still known as The Scholarship, because until shortly before I reached the age of eleven it provided exemption from fees of £5 a term at the local grammar school; but it represented, by the time I took it, the first flowering of the eleven-plus. Three schools in the area took children up to the age of eighteen. One of them was co-educational, a considerable distance from my home and so new that it had not had time to prove itself. The other two were the Harrow County Schools, one for boys and one for girls.

Harrow County School for Girls was very different from Greenhill Elementary. It was a two-storeyed brick building set in the pleasant grounds of a house which had been retained for the use of the sixth form and prefects. Although four concrete netball courts were laid down between the original block of classrooms and a new wing, the rest of the grounds still had the feel of a park, with mature chestnut and oak trees growing round what had become the hockey or rounders field. I had walked past it often, for it was next door to a recreation ground in whose pond I sailed my boats; whilst immediately in front of it was the steep and grassy slope of Harrow Hill, perfect for tobogganing in the snow.

My parents took it for granted that this was to be my destination, and I fervently hoped they were right: but as an anxious ten-year-old I had my doubts. Although there was a three-form entry totalling about ninety girls each year, Greenhill had never been known to supply more than two of these: and I knew that I was not the cleverest girl in the class. Mavis, the gentle daughter of a widow, had always beaten me in examinations, and more recently a girl called Peggy England had arrived from another school and immediately showed herself to be the superior of the rest of us. I could only hope that for once we could notch up three passes.

All the children who took the examination were well aware of its importance to our future lives. Although I feel quite sure now that my parents would have found some way of moving me away if I had failed, at the time a kind of mass hysteria gripped the whole class. I remember nothing of the test itself. Nor do I recall the letter which brought good news. But I have a vivid memory of my arrival at school to discover that I was the only girl to have been offered a place. Mavis was white-faced, shocked into speechlessness: Peggy did not come to school at all for the rest of the week.

The consequences of this early success have stayed with me for longer than I like. I am half ashamed of the opinions it engendered, and yet unable completely to free myself from them. From that experience grew not exactly an elitist attitude but certainly a belief in meritocracy. Given ambition, determination and hard work, surely anyone could succeed. Not necessarily in the academic field: it has always seemed important that parents and schools should open as many doors as possible to their children, and offer them a variety of ladders to climb. In terms of personal achievement, to be a pop star is as rewarding as to be a professor.

I admire people who, from a standing start, have translated ambition into achievement and I tend to feel that children who lack ambition and are content with day-to-day satisfactions will probably be as happy as they expect to be. But this theory makes little allowance for the child who is ambitious but lacks either the necessary talent or the determination which is often more important. Too many children are let down by their teachers. Far more suffer from parents who fail to recognise their own primary responsibility in the education of their offspring: and this creates a vicious circle when failed pupils become parents who care little about schooling and bring up more failing pupils in turn.

When my own first child was two years old Jeremy and I moved from a flat in Hampstead to a house in Teddington. Knowing nothing about the area, I set out to explore the educational possibilities. There were two state schools in our neighbourhood which accepted five-year-olds. The nearer of the two was a dead ringer for Greenhill. Built in the same decade, it had the same grim playground, the same high walls and even higher wire caging to keep in flying footballs. Its classrooms were shabby and the chilly lavatories were outside, across the playground. It took children up to the age of eleven, but its record of getting pupils through the eleven-plus was abysmal. No child of mine was going there.

A little further away was Bridgeman, for five to seven-year-olds only. Newly-built, it had been designed to the scale of its inhabitants: small desks, low lavatories and washbasins. The teachers believed -- as I did not -- in learning through play. But I knew that I could teach Jocelyn to read before she arrived, and the play atmosphere was friendly and welcoming. I wrote to the education office and put her name down for Bridgeman.

When the time came for her to start school and I joined the cluster of mothers waiting at the school gate an interesting fact emerged. The social segregation which is so much criticised when it results from private versus state education had established itself here between two state schools. One was filled by children whose parents had taken the trouble to investigate and to choose and to make sure that their choice was accepted. At the older school were those whose parents assumed that they must go where they were sent and that there was nothing to be done about it. One group of children would mainly achieve grammar school education: the other group mainly would not. Their paths had divided at the age of five: but it need not necessarily have happened like that.

I was fortunate in the first place to have parents who valued schooling and taught me to make the best of it. One result of this experience was the resolve to do the same for my own children later on. The most important use of my own education, it seemed to me as a young married woman, was to provide the early education of my daughter and son rather than develop a career; and it was a second stroke of good fortune that Jeremy could afford to support me in this.

Not everyone is as lucky. The child who has a goal and finds that the ladders are not wide enough has to face a personal tragedy at too young an age. Whenever I think smugly of my success as a scholarship girl, I have to remember my Greenhill classmates, whom I never saw again after I left the school. Did any of them manage to break out of that bleak building in some other way? Where are you now, Peggy England?

Little Mother

The winning of The Scholarship was not the only important event of my eleventh year, which also saw the birth of my sister Lauriston. This time I was well prepared: indeed, I began to get the impression that this baby was coming into the family mainly for my benefit. By the time she arrived my attitude was not so much that of Big Sister as Little Mother. I still had no liking for Hilary, who was in the irritating stage of non-stop chatter; but my feelings for Laurie were distinctly maternal.

This was convenient for my mother, who was forty years old and took a long time to recover from the birth. I was happy to bath the baby and put her to bed, and liked to read stories to her long before she was capable of understanding them. Every Saturday morning I pushed the high, heavy pram to the shops.

Shopping was a lengthy chore. More prosperous families had everything delivered -- and we of course patronised the baker and milkman whose horse-drawn carts came down the road every day -- but we needed the bargains offered by Pay'nTake. Sainsbury's was also reckoned to be good value, but required its customers to queue up separately at four or five counters, since it was clearly impossible for the same person to serve both bacon and cheese. As a ten-year-old I had to fight for attention from assistants who too often looked over my head to the woman behind. The experience made me in later life one of the earliest enthusiasts for supermarkets in which there are no shop assistants to hold service up by chat, and I can choose the piece of meat which looks best to me instead of relying on the kindness of a butcher -- who, after all, has to sell his toughest joints to *somebody*.

Lauriston's birth was an accident. With what always seemed to me great cruelty, although it was justified as honesty, this fact was never concealed from her. The effect upon Lauriston herself was that after her marriage she gave birth to seven babies, six of whom happily survived. The consequences in my own life and that of my parents were rather different.

I knew what was meant by this kind of 'accident'. My father's study was lined to the ceiling with bookshelves which were open to me without censorship and it had not taken long to learn that the most fascinating titles were kept on the highest shelf. '*Enduring Passion*', by Marie Stopes, proved not to be the romantic novel which its title suggested. It was in fact a sustained argument in favour of contraception, complete with diagrams of such items as Dutch caps. I may have been fuzzy about some of the details, but in general terms it was clear to me what had gone wrong.

Equally clear was the fact that my mother was reluctant to risk this kind of accident again. It was during this pregnancy that the matrimonial double bed was sold, to be replaced by a black lacquer bedroom suite covered with oriental figures standing on bridges or sitting under willow trees. I thought it was magnificent -- but noted at the same time that my parents were now sleeping in separate beds.

No child can know for certain what goes on in her parents' bedroom, but I feel fairly sure that the breakdown of the marriage of my father and mother dated from the unplanned birth of their third daughter. My mother's frequent references to the fact that all men are animals suggests that my father may have attempted from time to time to keep the relationship alive; but soon he found himself faced with a stronger defensive wall than the distance between two beds.

My mother became a sufferer from angina. I have no doubt that this was a genuine medical condition, and I know that it can cause spasms of excruciating pain. But a good many victims of the illness, carrying a bottle of pills in their pockets, manage to live ordinary, if careful, lives. My mother's reaction was to take to her (single) bed.

It was a gradual process. During the war years it would have been impractical for her to withdraw completely from the normal process of living -- and my father was hardly ever at home during that time. But for the last twenty years of her life she embraced the career of an invalid, leaving her bed only to walk to the bathroom and back. On one occasion she was taken to hospital suffering from pneumonia; and after treating her with oxygen and drugs the nurses insisted that she must sit in a chair for several hours a day, and walk up and down the ward for exercise. She should continue to do this, they told her firmly, after her discharge, and she would find that her condition improved. But they were talking to deaf ears. As soon as she was back in her own house she returned to bed.

It was a sad and prolonged ending to what had undoubtedly begun as a loving and happy marriage. The strength of my mother's religious feeling would have made divorce unthinkable for her, while my father was far too decent to abandon a sick woman. So for many years they lived separate lives in the same house. My mother could hardly bring herself to speak to her husband, who seemed to have accepted the situation without further protest. When I took my first baby over for inspection, I had sentimental hopes of seeing both grandparents cooing over her in the same room; but that was never to be the case. My time on every visit had to be precisely divided between the upstairs bedroom and the downstairs study.

Long before this state of affairs had been reached, my interpretation of the effects of that unwanted pregnancy on my parents had influenced my own thinking. I became -- and remain -- a vigorous supporter of the principle of contraception. 'Every child a wanted child' seems such an obviously desirable state that I feel any religion which outlaws efficient contraception to be not only mistaken but wicked.

More controversially, I go further than this in supporting the availability of abortion where contraception has failed, should the woman concerned wish for it. This may have something to do with my own child-bearing experiences. When, after a series of miscarriages, I produced my own first baby entirely as the result of medical intervention, this was viewed by society as laudable: why should it be any less acceptable to intervene in the opposite direction? Perhaps I have been influenced by the occasion on which my gynaecologist, away for the weekend, asked me to keep in the refrigerator a 17-week foetus which had just aborted naturally in my home until she could return to inspect it. This gave me long enough to stare at what might have become a baby but instead would never be anything more than a flawed part of myself.

If I state the belief that a foetus is part of a woman's body and that she is entitled to make her own choices about her body, no doubt science will say that I am wrong and royal commissions will reprove me as misguided; but it is far too late for me to change my views. I regard the creation of a new human life as a selfish act on the part of the parents -- which of course is not to say that it is wrong. The cutting off of that life before it begins is equally selfish -- which is not to say that that is wrong, either.

This attitude is not influenced by the undoubted affection which I felt for Lauriston. Had she never existed, she would never have been conscious that existence was possible; and I should not have grieved for a sister I had not expected to have. I may have exaggerated the consequences of her birth, because my mother's references to her own marriage in later years were not always to be believed; whilst my father never discussed such matters. But as an adolescent I observed what I believed to be the effects of an accidental pregnancy, and that observation had its effect on my own opinions.

Holidays at home

My father took his holidays abroad. As some compensation for having to work on Saturday mornings he was allowed six weeks' leave each year and spent much of that time cycling round Europe. On returning, he wrote travel books about his journeys; with titles like *Pedalling Poland* or *Ride to Russia*.

My mother would have liked to travel with him, although perhaps not on a bicycle. They did in fact have two or three walking holidays together: but five years after my birth they made a more ambitious journey to Corsica. A landslide on a mountain path came near to leaving me an orphan, and they were so appalled by the thought of this possibility that in future, they decided, one of them must always stay at home. This made little difference to my father, who enjoyed travelling alone. But my mother lacked social confidence and, after one lonely and unhappy expedition to Russia, she reconciled herself to holidays at home for a while. She was too fair-minded to blame the deprivation on me, but it was a factor in the resentment which she later developed against my father.

There was, however, a promised end to this period of self-denial. The idea of taking a young child abroad did not occur to either of them, but from as far back as I can remember I was promised a first trip across the Channel in 1940, as a fourteenth birthday present. The destination was to be the Passion Play at Oberammergau, performed every ten years. I looked forward to this eagerly; but of course in 1940 Oberammergau was hardly the ideal resort for British tourists. So I, like my mother, continued to spend holidays at home.

The holiday year had a fixed pattern. For a fortnight every summer, while my father was abroad, the rest of us travelled to Paignton, where my mother's father lived in retirement.

The Reverend David Donald had been born in Kirriemuir in 1866, near his friend J.M.Barrie. One of his first tasks after he started work was to escort a party of Dr Barnardo's orphans to Canada -- a fact which prompted me much later to read about the vogue for transporting orphans to the colonies, and to write *Lochandar*. Later he became a missionary with the Baptist Missionary Society, and it was while he was in the Lashai Hills, in northern India, that he had to deliver my mother and her twin sister when they were born prematurely. His wife died soon after the family's return to

England, so that his four children were brought up by a series of housekeepers while he worked as a Baptist minister. The household seems not to have been a very warm one, for my two uncles disappeared to Australia as soon as they could.

My mother had always assumed that devotion to the memory of his wife had prevented him from re-marrying, so it came as a shock to her when, with all the children off his hands, he married for a second time -- a much younger woman, who did not see herself as a grandmother and so required us to call her Auntie Ethel.

In spite of this disappointment, my mother adored her father and was not always tactful in making it clear that he was a saint while her husband was only an ordinary man. My own feelings were less enthusiastic. From the alacrity with which he disappeared into his study it was clear that Grandpa had no interest in children, but was merely doing his granddaughters a kindness by providing seaside accommodation. That was all right by us: it was the seaside we wanted. We spent most of the long train journey to Devon in the corridor, each hoping to be the first to catch the magical first glimpse: 'The sea! The sea!'

The nearest beach was Goodrington Sands, perfect for small children. I would be wearing a hand-knitted bathing costume, bright with stripes when dry, but pulled out of shape by the weight of water to hang round my knees after the first swim. We spent all day on the beach. My step-grandmother rented a chalet for the season, so we had shelter if it was wet; and every afternoon she would make her way down the winding cliff path through the steeply sloping beds of mesembryanthemums to make tea. Something which puzzles me is the memory that these beach meals always provided mouthfuls of sand, just as comic books about picnics promise; yet in my own later picnic-providing life sand has never been an ingredient nor even a threat.

Sometimes my father came to join us for the last day or two of the holiday. He took me once on an expedition to Brixham and gave me money to play at a fun-fair which had been set up on the edge of the harbour. I increased my stake by rolling pennies and setting little men to waddle through arches; and was not old enough to realise that this was not something to boast about in the Donald family. That evening proved a very frosty occasion. A man who encouraged his child to gamble was clearly not in the saint class.

I remember very little about my grandfather's home. This may be merely because our holidays there came to an end when the war put the coastline out of bounds to visitors. But I suspect that, like boarding-house landladies of the period, my step-grandmother may have made it clear that we should all stay out of the house between nine and five.

At Christmas it was the turn of my paternal grandmother to entertain us. My father had been born in Ibstock, surely the largest and ugliest village in Leicestershire, if not in the whole of England. It was a mining village; but most of the men who came out on strike in the year of my birth never worked again. They spent their days lounging against walls, half-cigarettes in their mouths. Their wives whitened doorsteps and black-leaded grates and scrubbed and polished with aprons over their faded dresses and their hair rolled tightly into steel curlers, ready to emerge as sausage-shaped curls in the evening.

My father was the youngest son of a large family, and the only one who got away from his birthplace, seeking his fortune in London. Those of his brothers who survived the Great War remained in Ibstock. Uncle Bill was the pork butcher of the village as his father had been -- and I was quickly made to understand that this was far more important than being an ordinary butcher; carrying with it as it did the redolence of rich pies and succulent sausages. Uncle Fred acted as a village solicitor, although in fact his qualifications, if any, were those of an estate agent. Uncle Harold had been born deaf and because of that was assumed from infancy to be ineducable. He was the village baker and his welcoming noises, above the roar of the flames, were a little frightening. Their children, all considerably older than myself, were unmarried and apparently content to spend the rest of their lives in Ibstock. They were first cousins, and yet I never established any kind of continuing relationship with them and lost contact completely as soon as my grandmother died.

Right from my first memory of her, Grandma seemed incredibly old. Her white hair was pulled back into a bun, her face was even more wrinkled than W.H.Auden's, and over a stiffening of several petticoats she invariably wore a full-length black dress, for she had been widowed while my father was still a boy.

In a village where everyone was poor, she was as poor in cash terms as any. Pride would not allow her to draw the pension to which she was entitled, so her sons supported her instead. But her house, double-fronted and detached, and raised above the road by tiers of rockery, was greatly superior to the terraced cottages of the miners. There was a lawn for outdoor tea, but most of the garden was devoted to vegetables and fruit.

My grandmother lived with a companion, who would have been her daughter-in-law had her son Arthur not been killed in the war. Auntie Mabel taught a class at school and ran the local Guides and Brownies, but was shamefully bullied at home as a reward for exceptional devotion. I had a soft spot for her because she twice took me on her Guide Camp, to Prestatyn in Wales, when I was only old enough to be a Brownie.

The two front rooms of the house were used only when there were visitors. The parlour, indeed, was never used at all. I was allowed to go into it occasionally, on Sunday afternoons, to study its treasures as though it were a museum -- which it greatly resembled. Above all else amongst its contents I coveted a suite of miniature furniture made out of feathers and protected by a glass dome. Grandma promised that she would leave it to me when she died. But when that time came she either died intestate or else left everything to be divided between her surviving children; and my mother, outraged that Auntie Mabel should get nothing after so many years of cheerful servitude, promptly handed over the whole of my father's share to her, without consulting anyone else. I don't think I would have been begrudged my feather furniture but didn't like to be too grabby about asking: and by the time I mentioned the matter it was too late.

On the other side of the front hall was the dining room, usually filled by a substantial mahogany table: but when we were there on holiday this was pushed against the window so that there was room for the family to sit round the fire. On her own, my grandmother spent all her time in the kitchen.

The kitchen was the largest room in the house, and the warmest. A double range burned day and night and a large and well-scrubbed table served for food preparation and meals. As a cook, my grandmother may have been limited in her range, but everything she produced was superb. Never in the forty-five years since her death have I tasted anything to rival the jellies she made from her own raspberries; her Yorkshire puddings, so light that they floated above the wide tin; and, above all, her nettle wine. I have spent many seasons of my adult life filling the house with the filthy smell of boiling nettles and then fermenting and fiddling with air locks, but have never been able to rival the sharp cool tang of my grandmother's vintages. As a Baptist family we were strictly teetotal: but country wines did not count and were even thought suitable for children: I can remember hot afternoons when I found it hard to walk in a straight line.

The bedrooms upstairs had to be juggled when we arrived. Auntie

Mabel gave up her room and retreated to a couch in a small sewing room, while Hilary and I sank into the depths of a real feather bed. I thought this to be the height of luxury, but at the same time sometimes felt as though I were suffocating. Remembering now how invariably on these visits I used to be ordered to stop sniffing, I sometimes wonder whether the hay fever from which I have suffered every summer took wing from those feathers.

Across the back of the house was a tiled area with a glass roof: it served both to raise seedlings and to dry clothes in wet weather. One door led from it to an open courtyard and the stable and coachhouse which served as our playroom during the holiday: the other opened into the laundry room.

I still shake my head in incredulity at the memory of those washdays. On Monday mornings Mrs Wilkins came to help, for the heavy linen sheets could hardly have been handled by a single person. The scrubbing and boiling and wringing and mangling processes took almost all day, with starching and drying and ironing still to come. Everything had to be ironed at exactly the right stage of dampness and with precisely the right degree of heat, for there were no easy-care fabrics. And until the mid-thirties there was no running water in the house.

Working the handle of the pump in the courtyard and carrying in buckets of water became one of my holiday tasks as soon as I was strong enough. But when I was ten or eleven we were greeted on our arrival with the news that water had arrived in the house. And not just in the kitchen and laundry room: for the first time there was a bathroom. Until then we had used basins of water on washstands; and chamber pots under the bed.

The new bathroom and lavatory were downstairs, and this posed a problem for any small person who needed them in the middle of the night. Blackie, the mongrel dog who stretched himself across the bottom stair, was friendly by day but had been trained to growl menacingly at anyone who disturbed him at night. After Hilary had an unfortunate experience, the chamber pots were returned to the bedroom.

My grandmother's working day was too full to allow her to play with us, but we were always welcome to help in the kitchen. And on Sundays she put on a different black dress, of a shinier material, and allowed herself an afternoon rest which was followed by a game of -- invariably -- Ludo.

My mother would have preferred to celebrate Christmas in her own home, where there would have been more emphasis on baby Jesus and less on food; but this was one point on which my father, in most ways amenable, could not be budged. Seen through the eyes of a child, it was a perfect traditional Christmas -- although it is certainly true that this is the only period of life in which I have felt sick from over-eating. Like getting drunk, this is something which perhaps has to be experienced once in order that a limit can be recognised. Even the war made little difference to the relentless parade of roasts and pies and hams: a butcher's mother was never likely to go hungry.

There were other traditions to be observed. A pile of pennies stood by the front door ready for the young carol singers who arrived almost in procession: those who knew the words of their carols right through were invited in for mince pies. There were tiny silver threepenny bits hidden inside the Christmas pudding, and I never understood how it was that the slices containing them always arrived on the plates of the children and not of the adults. There were Christmas stockings -- my father's old Army stockings -- swinging fat and rustling from the brass knobs at the end of the bed. The Father Christmas myth did not survive long in our family: it was so clearly my father who would wrap a tiny lump of coal in about twenty layers of paper -- all of which had to be unpeeled just in case it turned out to be a sixpence this year.

The contents of the stockings were cheap and cheerful -- a balloon, an orange, sweets, crayons, a handkerchief, something with which to make a noise. Proper Christmas presents could not be exchanged until after chapel and midday dinner and the king's afternoon speech on the radio. Other village families did not curb themselves in this way, and it was one of my early-morning delights on Christmas morning to watch children assembling on the field just across the road from the house. Almost all the girls sported some obviously new article of clothing. The boys wore their usual knee-length grey shorts, which always looked as though they had been bought to grow into or else handed down from a much taller brother -- there never seemed to be a moment when they were the right length. On Christmas Day one or two would have a new scarf or sweater, but the king of the day was the one who had been given a football. Even from a distance it was possible to be warmed by the happy glow of pride with which he exercised the privilege of choosing his team first.

The third school holiday of the year, at Easter, was usually spent at home, entertaining my mother's twin sister and her three sons; although on one occasion, shortly after Lauriston's birth, I went to their home in Newport instead. This too was a sternly Baptist household, but it was my cousins who introduced me to The Darkies' Sunday School, a irreverent song which did not go down well with my mother when I returned.

Solomon and David led most disgraceful lives.
They spent their time in making love to other people's wives.
Until at last their consciences began to give them qualms.
Then one wrote the Proverbs: the other wrote the Psalms.

The great excitement of staying with Auntie Dot was that the family owned a car. I loved being squeezed into the open dickie at the back for a ride to a picnic; but the holiday was not wholly delightful. I was bothered by the cane which hung prominently over the mirror in the dining room and which was used on the slightest pretext. As a visitor -- and a girl -- I was never caned by my uncle, but since I was always involved in whatever crime had been committed, I was made to watch the punishments being administered. My own father hit me only once in the whole of my childhood, and then only under orders from my great-aunt, whom I had kicked in a temper. His weapon was a bedroom slipper, and although I roared with indignation I was not in fact hurt: he rightly guessed that the rarity of the punishment would make me remember it for the rest of my life.

All these holidays were pleasant enough -- and anyway, I was hardly aware at first that any alternatives existed for anyone of my age. It was only because of my father's regular trips to Europe before the war that as I grew older I felt I was missing something, but the cheap package holiday for taking whole families abroad had not, I think, been devised. For children who did not have grandparents in the right places there were boarding houses and the first holiday camps: but at Greenhill Elementary most children were lucky to be offered an occasional Bank Holiday day trip, so in my early years I thought myself well off.

The collapse of the Oberammergau project, though, came as a considerable disappointment. As the war ground on and on and on, it seemed that I should never be able to explore the world: not, at least, until I was too old to enjoy it. I began to feel sulky in retrospect about the unchanging programme to which I had been condemned every year even before all frontiers had closed.

One predictable consequence of this was a determination to travel abroad as soon as it became possible; even before Europe had had time to pick itself up and rebuild its transport systems. The excitement of first visits to France and Italy in university vacations survived even the discomfort of train journeys on which the corridor floor provided the only sleeping space and all toilets were permanently occupied by passengers lucky enough to appropriate them as private compartments. After graduation I resolved to work overseas, and for a little while succeeded in doing so, combining a job in Egypt with holidays spent travelling alone in Syria, Jordan, the Lebanon and Cyprus. And with Jeremy's enthusiastic support, there has only been one year since our marriage -- when I had a young child and was pregnant again -- which has passed without a foreign holiday. We have been ruthless in leaning on kind relations or organising child exchanges with friends; and have never allowed the prospect of orphaning our children to deter us.

A less important effect has been the disinclination to return regularly -- or, indeed, at all -- to the same spot year after year; although perhaps our children might when they were young have liked the chance to set down secondary roots and make steady holiday friendships. They have both grown up to be adventurous travellers; so although something may have been lost, a good deal has been gained.

2

The war, which cut us off from holidays in my grandfather's seaside home, opened a different door. The time came when there were no longer enough able-bodied men to work on the land. Women of the Land Army filled the gap for most of the year, but there were not enough of them to fulfil the extra demands of harvest time. So a scheme was set up to send schoolchildren into the fields.

As can be imagined, this idea did not find an immediate welcome in the farming community. Children were scrumpers and poachers, and townees left gates open and allowed their dogs to worry sheep. To combine these two categories and let them loose on crops must have caused a good deal of moaning in country pubs. But Harrow County, as one of the schools to embrace the scheme with enthusiasm, set out to prove the grumblers wrong.

We were allotted an area round Temple Grafton, in the Vale of Evesham. For a month each year -- although no girl worked for more than two weeks at a time -- the village hall was placed at our disposal. In it we cooked and ate and dried our sopping clothes, while bell tents in a neighbouring field provided sleeping accommodation.

We were all suburban day girls, unused to community life and exhausting physical work, and not all the fifth and sixth formers in the first party chose to return in subsequent years. But for others it was a formative experience in many different ways.

I had read stories about boarding schools in books and magazines. Now for the first time I could enjoy midnight feasts and pillow fights and develop close friendships with girls outside my own year. The staff, too, were suddenly revealed as human beings as they struggled with communal cooking on unfamiliar appliances and charted the complicated arrangements of who should work where. Even the headmistress became a jolly friend as she played the piano for evening sing-songs.

Although we regarded the annual visits as holidays, there was very little free time. At the end of each working day we were too tired to do more than sleep. But Saturday afternoons were free, and some of us had brought our bicycles. Pedalling furiously up and down steep hills, we were able to reach Stratford in time to go to the theatre: here too I shakily learned to punt between dignified swans on an idyllic stretch of the Avon.

Sundays were special occasions. A harvest festival became a deeply moving occasion when we were the ones who had helped to bring in the harvest, and the traditional hymns can never have been sung with a more hearty sincerity.

The work was of several different kinds and varying degrees of popularity. Field work was the hardest. Picking up potatoes in the wake of a machine which turned over the earth to reveal them left us stooped like cripples, with aching backs, for the rest of the day. Picking peas had the effect of roughening the skin of the right forefinger and engraining it with an indelible greenish stain. Years of scrubbing were needed to remove the colour, and the roughness is there still.

Equally hard, but much jollier, was stooking. Sheaves of corn had to be tied, carried and stacked into wigwam-shapes to dry. Later, when the farmer pronounced them ready, they were pitchforked on to a cart, transferred to a barn or farmyard, and pitchforked again into a stack.

This activity caused our science mistress great anxiety. We were growing girls and could, she said, do ourselves irreparable harm by pitching a heavy weight upwards. To stack the sheaves up to shoulder level might not do much damage, but anything higher would endanger our chances of having children later on.

Needless to say, we took no notice of this warning. There was no one else to take over from us as the load on the cart grew higher; and the idea of giving birth to children was impossibly remote. The graceful movement of digging the two long, curved tines of the pitchfork into a sheaf and swinging it up into the air and off on to a stack provided a satisfying physical pleasure and the ride back to the farm on top of the swaying load was a fine reward -- as long as it did not overbalance on the way! When, eight years later, I started to miscarry in every pregnancy, Miss Philibert's warning returned to haunt me. It came as a relief to discover eventually that it was a hormone deficiency, and not some muscle over-strained in adolescence, which was to blame.

My own favourite activity was more dangerous but less arduous -- the picking of the plums for which the vale was famous. Until then I had thought of plums as being either Victorias or Others, but I soon became a connoisseur of local varieties: pick of the bunch was the Barton Belle.

The plum trees were tall and in order to reach the fruit two long ladders sloped from opposite sides to lock horns at the top. Our townee instinct was to make the slope as gentle as possible and we took a lot of persuading that the safest method was for the ladders to be almost vertical. Once they were in position and steady, two girls climbed, facing each other, at exactly the same pace and remained at an equal level before descending in the same way. We were beginners at this balancing act, and there were accidents from time to time, but since we usually fell into the trees rather than outwards, nothing too serious occurred.

A far greater hazard was posed by wasps. If we were to fill the punnets in acceptable time, our hands needed to move where our eyes could not always see. The slight squeeze and lift which tested whether a plum was ripe could prove aggravating to a wasp which had already made its decision on that point -- and most of the ladder accidents which did occur were caused by the involuntary jerk of reaction to a sting. No one wasted time on asking for or offering sympathy: these were our war wounds. They were treated by the application of gentian violet, a virulent purple stain: our war paint.

I attended three of these harvest camps and the consequences were simple and direct. I had never felt the slightest interest in tending the garden at home, although I was willing to weed if I were paid for it. But the growing of food seemed to me a marvellous thing: one of the best possible occupations. As the end of my schooldays approached, with the war still in progress, I announced that I wished to join the Land Army rather than one of the more glamorous women's services. It was the only occasion in my life on which my father said No: absolutely definitely No. I was entitled to go up to university for one year before being conscripted, if I chose, and that was what I must do. He himself had volunteered for the army in the Great War at the age of seventeen. By the time the war ended he felt the need to start earning and to marry; but he regretted for the rest of his life that he had never taken up his place at Cambridge. He was afraid that the same pattern might be repeated with me.

The war ended during my first year at university. so I never became a land girl; and the Hampstead flat in which Jeremy and I spent the first seven years of our married life did not boast even a balcony or window box. But once we moved to a house with a large garden, all my peasant instincts were revived. There was plenty of room to grow fruit and vegetables and a greenhouse in which to raise seedlings and perfect the art of ring culture for tomatoes.

Even that was not enough. In a moment of inspiration, Jeremy gave me as a birthday present one year four and a half acres of Sussex. It was an abandoned piece of land which had become separated from the large house which once owned it: there was no water and only the roughest access. In a neglected orchard apple trees rose from cones of brambles, promising unlimited helpings of blackberry and apple crumble to come. A sloping field was so densely covered with docks that it seemed wise never to let any neighbours know who owned it, lest the Weeds and Seeds Act should be hurled against us. But in the middle of this chaos was a walled garden.

Well, four walls, anyway, of grey Kentish ragstone. The large square they enclosed was, like the rest of the land, in appalling condition, but a proliferation of nettles suggested fertile soil beneath. I bought a Rotavator and set to work to turn it into a smallholding.

It was always too much for me to manage; and the long drive from Teddington to Ticehurst meant that once there, I worked for longer than was sensible. But I soon learned that with land to spare, vegetables will grow quite happily through a carpet of weeds, and before long was carrying off sacks of carrots and potatoes and parsnips and filling a large freezer at home with purees of blackcurrants and gooseberries as well as making jams and wines and leaving offerings on neighbours' doorsteps.

This venture had consequences of its own. There was no possibility of building a weekend cottage on the site, but it was surrounded by a group of large properties. They were originally built to care for mentally handicapped members of wealthy families, in healthy surroundings but out of sight of society. One of these houses had been converted into a residential hotel: it had a guest room which was available when the residents did not want it for their friends, and also a caravan in the grounds which could be rented. Since the amenities included croquet, table tennis and a cooked dinner, Jocelyn and Jonathan were happy to spend weekends with me there and to amuse themselves on our wild land. Round the outside of the walled garden were various derelict outbuildings, one of which Jonathan converted into a games room. Here he and Jeremy invented their own ball games, and I feel sure that his success in winning a half-blue as a fives player at Oxford had its roots in the Ticehurst pigsty.

The walled garden was the direct inspiration for two of my books. In *The Blow-and-Grow Year*, for children, the young heroine enjoyed the same pleasure as myself in clearing a neglected piece of land -- and was faced with the same alarm when an attempt to burn weeds blazed out of control. For adults, a novel called *The Girl Outside* used the exact setting of my own land, and even featured the pheasant whose visits used to give me so much pleasure.

After we moved to Kensington, the journey to Ticehurst through south London became a difficult one. Jeremy advised me to put the land out of mind in the hope that it might one day acquire a value under new planning rules. He was right, as the later building of a reservoir in the area suggested; but I couldn't do it. Even though I had never managed to keep the ground neat and tidy, to abandon it deliberately seemed almost as wicked as failing to care for a child. So it was sold to a neighbour to be preserved as a bird sanctuary.

That left me in a town house with only a tiny garden but an undiminished determination to keep digging. I wrote to the town clerk of Kensington, reminding him of his duty to supply his ratepayers with allotments. In a cheerful reply he pointed out the economic cost -- in rent and rateable value -- of growing a single row of potatoes in the royal borough itself, but offered me a plot somewhere near Heathrow.

This did not appeal, but help was at hand. A hockey-playing friend of Jeremy's was the tenant of an allotment at Barn Elms -- just south of the river, over Hammersmith Bridge. There was no possibility that I could rent one in my own name, since membership was confined to males who were resident in the borough of Richmond. But Noel had developed a bad back, and was under notice that he would have to give up his plot unless he could keep the weeds under control. I arrived ostensibly to help him, and in practice worked it single-handed. The fact that I was female and a non-resident was overlooked by the old gentleman who collected the rent every January, since Noel had the generous habit of wrapping the money round a bottle of whisky.

Working the plot was a daunting task. After an afternoon excavating weeds from the neglected soil I used to dream of the roots of couch grass, like thickly-tangled spaghetti. But little by little the ground came under control. The area was larger than I needed, and although I dutifully sowed for succession, every seed seemed to mature at the same time as its fellows. Jeremy began to complain that the year was divided into four seasons: those of leek soup, lettuce soup, courgette soup and tomato soup. I didn't take any notice. By this time the harvest had become less important to me than the process of working the land. Digging was to me what cycling had once been to my father: a time for thinking, with no one to interrupt. The routine of driving home a garden fork or spade and turning the earth, over and over again, makes no demands at all on the mind, which is set free to solve whatever problems have been put to it. The plots of all the novels which I wrote during our fourteen years in Kensington were worked out at Barn Elms.

When we left London after Jeremy's retirement, the allotment had to be relinquished. I found myself paying money for potatoes and parsnips for the first time in thirty years. Although it made sense to plan our new garden as a pleasant outdoor room rather than a very small smallholding, I was restless for the first winter. Should I apply for another allotment in Oxford? The garden itself, which we had taken over as a building site -- a sea of mud furnished only with nettles and bindweed and lumps of cement -- was providing enough work to be done for the time being, and I wasn't sure how much longer, as I grew older, I should be able to continue with the heavy digging which a vegetable plot needs. The answer seemed to be No.

My spirits were restored with the discovery of PYO. The middle of London is not well provided with pick-your-own farms, but suddenly we discovered ourselves to be surrounded by them. So now all the work of cultivating and planting-out and weeding and tying-in has disappeared, leaving only the delightful task of picking the choicest strawberries and raspberries and ignoring any mouldy or mis-shapen fruit. The black-fly on broad beans is somebody else's problem; and instead of collecting a few spears of asparagus each day in season until they add up to a helping, I can feed a whole dinner party generously and cheaply after half an hour in the farmer's large field.

Besides, even a small garden can make a contribution to the larder. In our own, peaches and plums grow against a wall, alpine strawberries and lettuces edge a border, and runner beans are as brightly decorative as clematis. You can't keep a good peasant up!

The cultivation of small plots of land is not the most glamorous of hobbies. It is a solitary pleasure, dirty and tiring. But if I measure my long harvest in terms of satisfaction, rather than simply in food collected and eaten, I know that all the seeds were sown in the harvest camp at Temple Grafton. This was for me one of the happier consequences of the Second World War.

Playtime

The first outdoor activity which I remember with affection was playing with boats. At first this entailed an escorted walk to a small park. In its pond a flat-bottomed barge could be pulled round on a string. But as soon as I was old enough to go off by myself, my destination would be the rec., a large recreation ground. As well as grass areas for football this contained all the usual slides and swings and see-saws. It also had a good-sized boating pond to which, as the years passed, I carried a series of ever bigger yachts. I have a faint memory of once owning a motor boat which was powered by camphor, but sailing boats were the favourite, even though there could be anxious moments when the wind dropped and the yacht was becalmed out of reach.

If these holiday mornings had any influence on my future hobbies, it showed itself only when I was working in Egypt, on the shore of the Great Bitter Lake. For a year I had a half share in a Snipe. The wind pattern was most satisfactory: whatever its direction for most of the day, it always blew back to shore at five o'clock, enabling us all to race back to the clubhouse with spinnakers billowing. The experience was just about adequate for me to allow one or two of the characters in my novels to sail, but did not survive the return to England. Although I have never since then lived far from the Thames, river sailing seems unexciting.

There were no worries in those pre-war days about letting children roam where they liked. Not too far from home were the green slopes of Harrow Hill. The fields were mostly owned by the school and used for games, but footpaths ran through and there seemed no objection to anyone else playing there. A friend and I would take our ball to the rugger ground, but our real pleasure was to play on the grandstand.

This was a simple wooden structure supported by vertical and horizontal beams which made it a perfect climbing frame. We could swing from its higher beams or turn somersaults on the lower ones, no doubt displaying our knickers in the process. Very often an elderly man came to watch us, unbuttoning his trousers as though the field were a public lavatory. We thought he was rude (and in our vocabulary 'rude' was a very strong adjective, which had nothing to do with good manners) but it never occurred to me to mention him to my parents and he never came close. Years later, reading an incredible statistic about the proportion of the population which has been 'abused' in childhood, I read the small print definition of abuse with care and discovered that my visits to the grandstand would qualify me for inclusion. But in an age when children took it for granted that most people, even strangers, were friendly, there was no need to be frightened. Innocence might not have been a true protection, but it felt like one.

In a field grazed by horses a little lower down the hill, where Northwick Park Hospital now stands, was another pond. Not lined with concrete like those in the park and the rec., but a proper muddy pond. Here we would fish for newts. Some were ordinary newts and some, because of their fine markings, we called (perhaps correctly, perhaps not) emperor newts. We carried them triumphantly home in jam jars, together with frog spawn in season. But there was another treasure to be found in the pond, for on the far side of a hedge was a golf course. Dredging the mud with our fishing nets we could usually expect a good haul of golf balls, to be sold back to the club. Pocket money was extremely low, so all additional sources of income were welcome.

Winter brought its own activities. The steepest slope of the hill, when covered with snow, was perfect for tobogganing -- even though my toboggan was only the usual tin tray. And freezing weather meant that the Ruislip Lido, on which in summer I used to row, became an outdoor skating rink.

I learned to skate when I was twelve. Sessions at the nearest rink, in Wembley, replaced Saturday fleapit film matinées as a regular winter activity. It's difficult to recall why I enjoyed it, because I couldn't afford lessons and never learned to dance on ice in more than a clumsy way, or to manage more than the simplest figures. Even going backwards, although easy, could not be practised for long because of the danger of collisions. So most of the time was spent speeding round and round. But the music was cheerful and there was an atmosphere of excitement which gripped me as soon as I began to lace up my skates and make my cautious way over the boards and on to the ice.

Skating out of doors was quite different. With no canned music, it was possible to hear the singing of the blades on the ice. There was more room to manoeuvre and to move in any direction. The contrast between a chilled face and a warm body was invigorating and there was a good feeling of doing something natural and seasonal: I have always liked seasonal activities just because they come to an end and so can be looked forward to again.

Games at school were equally seasonal -- not at Greenhill, where there was no room for anything but drill, but at Harrow County. In summer we played rounders. This seems to me such a suitable game for keeping all members of two teams actively involved throughout a match that I have never been able to understand why schoolboys are made to play cricket instead, poor things.

The spring term was devoted to netball. When I first arrived at the county school, hockey was the autumn game; and I very much enjoyed it. Women's hockey, unlike the male version which I watched after marrying a hockey player, tends to be a fluid game, not often interrupted by the whistle. I was never a fast runner, but had sufficient stamina to keep on the move for as long as required. By the age of fifteen I had hopes of gaining my school colours; but then a new games mistress arrived.

She declared that hockey was bad for growing girls, who ought not to keep their heads down and their shoulders hunched over a hockey stick. Instead, she overnight changed the school over to lacrosse in order that our chests could expand and our breathing and posture improve. I was one of the many who sulked at the change and refused to make any effort in the unwanted new game.

There was little room for tennis in this annual timetable, although in summer the netball courts were given a new set of lines. The threat of air raids after the start of the war made it undesirable for many activities to go on after school, so the only tennis coaching on offer took place in the lunch hour -- and only for a select number of girls who were thought to be possible candidates for a school team. The games mistress and I were not best friends, and so I was not one of them. I resented that at the time, and resent it still. When I married Jeremy, who was a good player, I joined a tennis club with him and have played the game regularly ever since; but if I had ever actually been taught to play, instead of picking it up as I went along, I'm sure I could have done much better.

Of all the outdoor activities on offer, my favourite was cycling. The freedom to roam which had taken me to the rec. or the Harrow fields before I was eleven, extended to the whole country when I was in my teens. My father, who liked to have me as a companion, had very early accustomed me to riding distances which were long for my age; so when I took off with my best friend in the school holidays, we set our ambitions high. Eighty miles a day was the norm and ninety was possible. Once or twice we planned on a hundred, but usually had to hitch a lift if we were to achieve it. (As with the grandstand episode, it never even crossed our minds that any of the helpful lorry drivers who stopped to pick us up might wish to harm us.) We stayed at youth hostels, carrying the compulsory sleeping bags -- made out of a sewn-up sheet in my case -- and most of the food we would need. The cost was extremely low, although kitchen chores were part of the fee.

I don't remember that we ever did any sightseeing in the places we visited. The enjoyment lay in covering the distance and arriving at a planned destination; experiencing a county in terms of its scenery and gradients. Roads in those days were relatively safe for cyclists. Cars were driven much more slowly than today; and during the war, petrol rationing meant that not many of them were on the road at all.

It was a great disappointment that I was never able to share this particular pleasure with my own children. By the time they were old enough to want to cycle to school, it seemed to me that there were far too many junctions on the way in which there was simply no safe place for a cyclist. Refusing to buy them anything larger than a fairy cycle went very much against the grain, but was one of the few prohibitions which I refused to relax until Jonathan started at Winchester. There, though, it was compulsory to have a bicycle and the roads therefore had to be considered safe. Since he was twelve by then, his crash course in learning to ride did indeed include a few crashes. I do realise, of course, that it is people like me who enjoy driving -- millions of us -- who have made it so hard for our own children to enjoy cycling.

2

Outdoor activities were the most exciting, but there were plenty of absorbing hobbies at home.

Although for a year or two my beloved bedtime companion was a rag Dutch girl with yellow plaits, I didn't as a general rule rate dolls highly as playthings. But after I came out of hospital at the age of six, my father made me a dolls' house. He was not a skilful handyman, and it was an extremely basic residence: a wooden chest sliced in half to provide a back with floor, ceiling and two side walls and then divided with plywood into four square rooms. There was no front; but the roof was covered with paper in the pattern of tiles and the sides with a pattern of bricks, so there could be no doubt that a dolls' house was what it was.

Too large to stay in my bedroom, it was kept up in the cold attic. I liked playing with it because everything had to be miniature and because I had to decorate and furnish it myself. Oddments of cloth served as carpets, furniture was made out of matchboxes, food and ornaments were plasticine and the inhabitants themselves were round-headed clothes pegs dressed in more scraps from the sewing box.

My pleasure in moving the peg family around was only exceeded by the delight of being given a Pollock's Toy Theatre three or four years later. In this the characters were paper, pasted on to card and manipulated on wire rods; but there was no longer any domestic limit to their adventures. Cinderella can rarely have led a more exciting life.

Another toy which lived in the attic was my train set, which was presumably like everyone else's train set of the Thirties. Engines were wound up with keys and rails were slotted into each other with prongs which frequently slid apart to cause derailments. I knew that electric trains existed, because I had been taken to Beaconscot to see the miniature village through which trains ran smoothly all day. But these were superior to mine by so many degrees that they were outside the range of covetousness.

Painting was another pleasure until Mr Shaw, the Greenhill art master, came along to knock it out of me. It was a great excitement to be given a huge paintbox with dozens of tiny rectangles of colour; but in practice water colour proved insipid. The real treat was to use poster paints, learning from experience what colours could be created by mixtures of the powders. My designs were not so much bright as gaudy and I had a taste for outlining every section in black, like stained glass. Had I ever heard of Rouault, I would have recognised him as a kindred spirit.

The pleasure of making furniture for the dolls' house led later to the more demanding hobby of constructing model aeroplanes; but the excitement here tended to be bitter-sweet. A glider was simple and safe enough, but I set my ambitions higher, making complicated machines out of fragile balsa wood and even matchsticks. They were powered by turning the propeller to twist an elastic band, but there was no way of controlling the plane to land safely, so that all too often hours of work crumpled in the first crash.

More lasting, at a later age, was a craze for making stools. The wooden framework could be bought ready-made. Painstakingly I would prime the wood, paint it and varnish it before weaving what I think was called sea-grass -- a tough twine -- in colour patterns to form the top. Most of these I gave away or sold on, but one is still around somewhere in the family more than fifty years later: a tribute to its long-lasting quality.

Like the sorting of marbles or arrangement of cigarette cards in albums, most of these hobbies were solitary ones. The six-year gap before the arrival of a sister gave me a long period of being in the play sense an only child. But there was one period a week, after Sunday School and tea, which was devoted to a family game. In the early days it was usually Rummy; but later Monopoly took over. My mother, who liked to give money away rather than acquire it, was reduced almost to tears by the hard-hearted glee with which I or my father would demand rent on a hotel in Mayfair.

The train set has left no lasting mark on my life. The toy theatre may have encouraged my later ambition to be a playwright; but since this never came to anything, the encouragement was clearly insufficient. My talent for Monopoly did not turn me into a grasping landlady. But the more practical activities do seem to have steered me in the direction of becoming a DIY enthusiast. After bookshops and garden centres, DIY supermarkets provide my favourite browsing shops: there are few excitements in the world of shopping to beat the discovery of a toggle-plug which will enable a huge weight of books to be stored safely on a plasterboard wall.

So now as an adult I paint and paper walls and ceilings and put up shelves to carry our ever-increasing store of books. When Jonathan, while abroad, acquired his first flat, I constructed whole ranges of furniture out of flat-pack boxes. Fixing a high bridging unit between two wardrobes was a distinctly more demanding matter than glueing matchboxes together to provide peg dolls with a comfortable bedroom suite; but a direct descendant of the process, all the same.

Of all my indoor occupations, though, the most important was reading: and that was a life in itself.

Windows on the world

Everyone gave me books for Christmas when I was young: I was disappointed if they didn't. My mother chose anthologies of verse, while my father fed me with information. Starting with *The Wonder Book of Why and What*, I built up a collection of Wonder Books over the years; while another favourite, *Romance of the Nations*, provided a fascinating introduction to social history. A complete series of the Myths and Legends of various countries read as excitingly as fiction -- which perhaps it was.

My grandmother chose books from a list recommended for Sunday School prizes. Many of these were old-fashioned even in the 1930s, but the collection did contain *Pollyanna* and *What Katy Did*, both remembered with affection. I also won Sunday School prizes in my own right. A Baptist organisation which provided a daily diet of Bible readings also held an annual Bible competition which required little more than the ability to memorise the prescribed texts. The winner was allowed to make her own choices, and there were some raised eyebrows in the Baptist congregation one year when I decided to spend my ten-shilling prize on twenty books by G.A.Henty, price sixpence each.

A more eccentric choice of reading came from my grandmother's companion, Auntie Mabel. She was incapable of resisting the sales talk of door-to-door salesmen who offered sets of books bound in blue and gold: but having acquired these, she did not particularly want to read them and so doled them out as gifts, one or two volumes at a time. From this source I acquired part-sets of Kipling, Dickens and Jeffrey Farnol, before pleading for a different system of division and managing to collect a complete Galsworthy.

Most of my fiction reading necessarily came from libraries; but the public library in Harrow was small and only opened at awkward hours; so instead I was allowed to choose books on my father's ticket at Boots' lending library. There were no picture covers to attract interest: all books were bound in the same style in one of four or five plain colours, with a shield-shaped sticker on the front and a brass-edged hole in the spine to take the tag which was part of the record of borrowing.

Later, when I was about eleven, a large new public library was opened at Kingsbury. It was about an hour's walk each way and its size posed a problem. I felt too old for the children's section but there was no way of knowing what might be of interest on the adult shelves. After one disappointing visit -- when I chose a title by a familiar author, Richmal Crompton, only to discover after I had lugged it home that it was a soppy love story -- I formed the habit of skipping through the first chapter of each choice before leaving the premises. Reading in the library became a regular pleasure.

All this time, of course, I had a lending library closer at hand, and took full advantage of it. My father filled his house with books. They covered the walls of his study from floor to ceiling. They spread to the hall and drawing room and crept upstairs to the attic.

As with the public library, I was left to forage in this treasure-house for myself. Books considered unsuitable for my age, such as *Tom Jones*, were positioned on the top shelf of the study -- easily reached by standing on a chair -- but there were no formal restrictions. Reading Upton Sinclair's *The Jungle* far too young, under the impression that such a title must indicate a children's book, I absorbed a tear-stained introduction to tragedy and social injustice. The short stories of O.Henry inspired me to turn all my school essays into elaborately-constructed masterpieces of twist and double-twist. Jean Webster and Ian Hay provided strong, silent heroes for romantic moods; Leacock and W.W.Jacobs made me laugh; Raffles represented crime. Nothing on offer was newly-published: I was reading my way through the choices of an earlier generation.

These books furnished my childhood just as they furnished my home. But when my father died, he left all the contents of his home to my stepmother. One Sunday morning, she rang me up.

'Someone's coming round in half an hour to make an offer for the books. Are there any you'd like before he takes them away?'

There was no time to waste on indignation at the shortness of the notice. Perhaps she hadn't realised how important the matter was to me. It was a forty-minute drive, but I arrived on the doorstep at the same time as the bookseller, and for the first few minutes we raced each other round the shelves, each staring suspiciously whenever the other stretched out a hand. Then we both began to laugh as we realised that we weren't in competition. He was looking for treasure: I was only trying to dig out old favourites.

There wasn't much treasure. With time to look around, I realised how shabby the whole collection was: for a simple reason. Except for a few school prizes and a collection of political pamphlets which had come hot from the press in the 1930s, my father bought all his books second-hand. Many of them still sported the Boots shield, with a thick black cross to prove that the book had been sold off at the end of its lending life. But far more of them bore on the fly leaf a pencilled price -- 2d, 3d, 6d, even very occasionally 1/- -- in the neat writing of Mr Shepherd. Or perhaps he was Mr Shepheard: I can't remember the spelling, but I shall never forget the shop.

A visit to Shepherd's was one of my great Saturday treats. It was not in the main shopping area, but instead faced a busy road junction where a bridge crossed one of the main railway lines to Scotland. It was not really a shop, in fact, but a house. Possibly Mr Shepherd did live at the very top of it; but every room on the three lowest floors was lined with books. There were bookcases up the sides of the staircase, and more books piled on the stairs themselves, so that moving up and down required care.

The rooms were allocated to subjects, but the stairs housed comparatively recent arrivals, awaiting distribution. While my father browsed in the sections which interested him, I sat on the stairs; and when he left, I stayed on. Only once or twice a year could I afford actually to buy anything, even for only twopence, but Mr Shepherd never seemed to object when I used his stairs as a reading room.

There were two separate pleasures to be indulged. As well as enjoying the contents of the books and being constantly amazed by the variety of subjects, I enjoyed reading the bookplates and inscriptions and trying to imagine the houses and families from which each volume had come. I dipped into anything which caught my eye, but there were two subjects above all which came to fascinate me, so that I began to look them out. All reading must have consequences of one sort or another, if only in affecting an attitude of mind: but these two subjects proved to have more than a passing interest.

The first of them was the Great War. My father had fought in it, and found it so horrifying that although he could write on military subjects, he could never bring himself to talk about his war experiences. A puzzling part of my childhood routine was that I was expected to accompany him once a year to see an old comrade of his who now lived in St Bernard's Monastery. The friend greeted us with smiles, but never spoke a word during the visit. Since I had heard of Trappist monks, this did not surprise me at first, but I gradually became aware that his was not a silent order: he would have been allowed to talk if he wished. It had to be explained to me that he had been shell-shocked into silence. The reason for my participation in the visits was so that my father could keep a conversation going with me, allowing his friend to continue the nods and smiles. But the conversation never dwelt on the experience they had shared.

So even when I was quite young -- eight or nine -- I was curious about the war and wanted to know exactly what had made it so horrible. I found all the answers two or three years later on Mr Shepherd's staircase, in volumes of memoirs, letters, war poetry. As a picture of the Battle of the Somme built up in my mind, I felt it was too terrible to be true, and yet that it certainly must be true.

Then something even more hideous emerged. I came across bound volumes of *The Anzac Magazine*. Working out what Anzac meant took a little time, and at first -- because there were a good many cartoons and crude drawings -- I assumed that I was looking at a kind of comic annual. But gradually I was able to work out the nature of the Gallipoli campaign from the comments -- often bitter but sometimes funny -- of the men who fought it.

I was left with a strong feeling that one day I would like to write about that war -- almost as a memorial to the men who died in it, as an indication that a later generation had not forgotten them. When -- very many years later -- I was invited to write a family saga, covering a period of a hundred years, one of the attractions of the idea was that I would be able to write a novel about the Great War which might gain depth from the fact that the characters would have had time to establish themselves in their lives before the war began: and those who survived would return to tackle the problems of peace. Naturally I had to do a lot of detailed reading before I sat down to write *Lorimers at War* and the Gallipoli chapters of *Lochandar*, but the most vital piece of research -- because it had inspired the desire to write -- took place on Mr Shepherd's staircase.

That was a merely literary by-product of my browsing. But the discovery of another book on the staircase had a direct consequence in shaping the way I wanted to live.

The book which affected me so strongly was falling to pieces. The red cover had come apart from the pages, and the string and glue which held the sections together were also breaking up. Between each reading session I used to conceal the volume between the banisters and the piles of books so that no one would buy it before I had finished; but probably there was not much danger of that. I bought it myself in the end, for threepence. It was John Stow's *Survey of London*.

The streets it described were very different from the suburb in which I lived. When my parents made their ambitious move into 3 Gerard Road, it offered everything they wanted for a young family, and they both continued to live there until they died.

Although it was semi-detached, the house was spacious by later housing standards. Behind the inevitable privet hedge was a small front garden, never in any sense used: its purpose was to set the house back from the pavement and if possible to impress the neighbours. At the side a wide drive led to a garage which my father let out, since we owned no car. A smaller shed housed bicycles and pram. The back garden, a dull rectangle with straight paths down each side between the lawn and a narrow flower bed, held little excitement for older children, but it was large enough when I was a little girl, pitching my tent on the grass and sleeping outside with the spiders.

Inside the front door, a square hall and a wide, turning staircase gave an uncramped welcome. The front room became my father's study later on, but for almost ten years of my childhood we had a lodger: Great-Aunt Agnes. As well as one of the bedrooms, and a kitchenette which was specially built on to the side of the house, she used what should have been the family's dining room as her sitting room. At the back, with French doors to the garden, was a very spacious room which I would now call the drawing room but which was then always the lounge: it easily absorbed a baby grand piano in one corner, as well as containing all the expected sofas, arm chairs and bookcases.

Because we had lost the dining room to Great-Aunt Agnes, family meals were taken in the breakfast room, which should have been the kitchen; leaving the cooking, washing and washing up to be done in a tiny area which should have been only a scullery. With no refrigerator, no washing machine and no thermostats to keep the iron or the gas cooker from overheating, my mother had little help with the household chores.

There were four bedrooms on the first floor; two of them small. My parents, to begin with, shared a large, light front bedroom. The second double room, which had a wide verandah, was used by my great-aunt. When she left in 1938, fearing war and bombing, the verandah was converted into two tiny rooms. This was not very successful, since it made the original bedroom dark. For a time, when an Austrian Jewish family took refuge with us, I had to move into the inner verandah room, and this involved passing through Hilary's cubicle to reach it. Neither of us thought much of this arrangement. For most of my childhood, though, I was lucky enough to have a room to myself. My mother did her best to keep the family together in the evenings, but my father and I each retreated to our own dens, to write books or do homework.

A proper staircase led up from this floor to the attic, a large room whose ceiling sloped with the shape of the roof. The builder probably intended this for a servant, but it was always very cold and the four beds it could hold were made up only when my cousins came to stay. At other times it was ideal for setting up railways or making models which would not need to be cleared away between each session.

The attic was particularly cold, but the rest of the house was not much warmer. I felt no sense of deprivation at the lack of central heating, since I was unaware that such a thing existed: no one I knew enjoyed that particular luxury. If we complained that we were freezing, the remedy was to wear more vests or jumpers. But at least until the falling of the wartime bomb which cracked our back boiler, the breakfast room fire was rarely allowed to go out. As tyrannical as some elderly relation, it demanded constant attention and forbade prolonged absences: but like a cunning nurse my mother became adept at stoking up and damping down; so that although we shivered in our bedrooms, breakfast was a cosy meal.

When the breakfast room fire could no longer be safely used, an electric fire was bought which could be moved from room to room. For a time the only alternative source of warmth was the coal fire which was lit in the lounge every Sunday afternoon in the winter. But when I was about fifteen a tiny gas fire was installed in my bedroom so that I could do my homework in some degree of comfort. It wasn't large or efficient enough to warm the whole room, so I took to sitting close in front of it with legs apart and soon developed on my calves brown blotches which I feared would disfigure me for life. The bills which nowadays give us the freedom to move anywhere in the house and still be warm seem to me to be well worth paying.

I suspect that any family in the nineteen-nineties which shivers in a cold house and lacks television, washing machine, refrigerator and hot water would be considered deprived. But the definition of poverty in England has become a relative matter, linked more to levels of expectation than to hunger. In the nineteen-thirties I was well aware that, compared to most of the Greenhill Elementary pupils, I had a comfortable home.

As for the area in which the house stood, it was quiet and pleasant. The houses further along the road had been built later than ours -- I can remember playing in the piles of builders' sand and discovering with surprise that it was much dirtier than the contents of my own tiny sandpit. These newer houses were detached and expensive: our near neighbours included a bank manager, the manager of a shipping line, a lawyer and a headmaster. Most of them took the same daily walk as my father, to Northwick Park station, which offered both Metropolitan and Bakerloo line trains into Baker Street. They all left home at about ten past eight: they all arrived back at about ten to six.

There was a good secondary school within cycling distance -- and so few cars on the side roads that cycling was safe, even with 'no hands!' There was a thriving Baptist church community which provided my parents with all the social life they wanted. There were plenty of trees, and the feeling that other greenness was not far away. There was, indeed, a great deal to be said for suburban life. But without knowing why, I decided at a surprisingly early age that I didn't like it.

There have been long periods in which it has been fashionable to sneer at the suburbs, but I was not exposed to intellectual affectations and would never have known anything about that. At other times the many virtues of suburban life have been accorded full value, for without doubt they provide a healthy atmosphere in which to bring up children; and I must have recognised that in many ways I was fortunate to experience such an upbringing. I really don't know why it was that I took against Harrow before even reaching my teens; but I determined that as soon as I was old enough I would leave the area and never return -- an ambition which I fulfilled with relish.

Harrow-on-the-hill, of course, could not properly be described as a suburb: but we lived at the foot of the hill, and the difference was very clear. I often walked up the hill, where the old church had a marvellous position.

The terrace of the churchyard was an ideal spot in which to write the death-dominated poems in which I specialised as an adolescent -- and from a rather better poem carved into a tombstone I learned that Byron, as a Harrow schoolboy, had found the ambience as inspiring as I did.

The buildings of Harrow School dominated the top of the hill, and I was sufficiently impressed by them to recognise that Harrow-on-the-hill was a proper place in a way that Harrow-below-the-Hill was not. But that didn't mean that I liked it. Its high pavements were dominated by arrogant youths in absurd costume who expected the townees to step down into the gutter when they approached, three or four abreast. If you stood your ground, they pushed. In the matter of good manners, there was not much difference, I thought resentfully, between them and the roughies of Greenhill Elementary School. (Minor consequence: I would never have allowed any son of mine to go to Harrow.)

This is a very long interlude to explain why I was bowled over by the battered red book whose pages were continually trying to escape. By the age of eleven or twelve I had felt for some years that there was something unsatisfactory about living where I did, although I didn't know what it was. What I *thought* was missing was any opportunity for the kind of adventures enjoyed by Arthur Ransome's Amazons, or Alan Breck or Huckleberry Finn. Now, with the help of John Stow, I discovered the true lack. Gerard Road had no history.

Many years earlier, as I sat beside my mother at the piano, our normal repertoire of Sunday School hymns (*Hurry, pennies, hurry, though you are so few*) had been augmented by a book of songs based on London names. *Things are dear on this side, things are cheap on that: I shall shop on the Cheapside when I buy my Saturday hat,* was one; and, more dramatic, with crashing chords as accompaniment, *King's cross! What shall we do? His purple robe he's rent in two. Out of his crown he's torn the gems; he's thrown his sceptre into the Thames. The court is shaking in its shoe. King's cross! What shall we do? Leave him alone for a minute or two.* (The temptation to quote as a test of memory, sixty years on, is irresistible.)

Stow's explanations of how London streets had acquired their names was rather more scholarly and utterly enthralling. At first my explorations had to be mainly confined to the printed page. Although before the war I was regularly taken to South Kensington, to visit the museums clustered there, I was not familiar at all with the City of London, and now learned for the first time about its guilds, and the reasons why streets were named for the crafts which were practised and the goods once traded there. I studied maps in order to trace old walls and watercourses and identify gates and fords. Working backwards on my own account, I acquired a modern street map and invented explanations for street names unknown to Stow. It is difficult to make this sound as exciting as it felt at the time.

A more practical form of exploration began during the war, when I was fourteen. The Blitz had started. My mother was in the country with Hilary and Lauriston and my father was continually on the move as a Ministry of Information lecturer. He would call at home about once a fortnight and very often would ask me to go up to Malet Street on a Saturday to return books to the University of London library and to collect others which he had ordered. This seems an odd errand to suggest to a fourteen-year-old during the months when bombs were falling, but it must have been a period when all air raids took place at night, for neither he nor I felt nervous about the arrangement.

I was given my train fare and there was no one to worry about the time of my return. After exchanging the books I set off to discover the streets whose names I had studied. On at least one occasion I was turned back because they were burning, and on several other days I found myself climbing over rubble or crunching through shattered glass. But it was the beginning of a hobby which continued over many years; and as I paced the streets and consulted my bible, its red cover by now pasted over with amateur attempts at bookbinding, I developed a deep love of London.

It was a fashionable emotion. The government, which had originally feared panic when the bombs started to fall, were putting a great propaganda effort into the theme of 'London can take it'. The whole country was exhorted to admire the way in which Londoners were determinedly surviving every attempt to drive them out; and Londoners themselves were encouraged to be proud of the way they survived chaotic transport, sleepless nights and the continuing fear of homelessness, bereavement, injury or death. I shared in that feeling of pride: but there was a problem. I was not actually a Londoner.

The consequence of John Stow's influence on my adolescent years was a predictable one. As soon as I could get away from home, I intended to live in London; to become a Londoner.

In the event I only managed to achieve this for twenty-one years, but they were good years. A flat in Hampstead and, later, a house in Kensington confirmed my Stow-induced belief that the city still consists of a collection of villages. At the same time, a capital city contains so many national monuments and the headquarters of great enterprises that it offers all the exhilaration of being at the centre of things. To visit the city from outside, or to travel in daily to work, can be tiring and even depressing, as I know from being a provincial myself now: but to be an insider, a resident, is a continuing delight. *A Clean Break*, the novel I wrote after ceasing to live in London, was a valediction which came from the heart.

In addition to that particular chapter of education, Stow's *Survey of London* had a more general consequence. In the course of suggesting to me what it was that a suburb lacked, it encouraged me to make myself receptive to the spirits of places. And on almost every occasion when a place has in a sense forced its identity into my mind, I have felt compelled to write a novel which makes use of that power.

These recognitions are certainly not personal to me. The stadium at Delphi, a mansion in Natchez left unfinished since the start of the Civil War, a gallery carved from the rock of Petra, a medieval lane in Oxford, a temple at Ellora -- places like these must exert an influence on many of the visitors who allow time there for quietness. But not on all: so whenever I feel myself overwhelmed and inspired by the spirit of a place, I trace the course of my pleasure in it back to the staircase of Mr Shepherd's bookshop.

Places where they sing

My mother believed in home education. She taught me to read when I was three, and I have always been grateful to her for opening the world of books to me at such an early age.

She also -- as many other mothers do for their children, no doubt -- introduced me to verse. I read it, wrote it and memorised it. In later life she used to boast about the many thousands of lines which I could quote by the age of seven. Her belief at the time was that she was training my memory, but I have ruefully come to suspect that in fact this exercise may have used up all the memory cells I was born with, leaving me few to use in later life. I can still, if requested, proclaim the fact that *Christopher Robin goes hoppity, hoppity, hoppity, hoppity, hop* -- and so on and so on; but find it rather more difficult to recall the name of someone to whom I was introduced an hour ago. I enjoyed the exercise at the time, however, and have continued to read poetry and write verse throughout my life; so this is a second cause for gratitude.

Less successful was the decision that I should be taught French at home. Our lodger, my Great-Aunt Agnes, was a retired headmistress in her seventies, and short of occupation. Her offer to teach me was accepted eagerly by my parents but sulkily by myself. If I was expected to learn extra subjects and do homework, then I ought to have been allowed to go to cerise-blazered Heathfield School. There were perpetual battles on the subject, and my childish resentment may explain the fact that although I can read French I am incapable of holding a civilised conversation in that language.

The books from which I was taught featured a family of mice. *Madame Souris a une maison*, the first one began. *La maison de Madame Souris a quartre fenêtres.* The series continued through several volumes, but the page which brought me to a full stop included a picture of the mice-children being bombed. I still find it extraordinary that such a concept should have been included in a book for young readers. Presumably it was intended as some kind of anti-German propaganda, but I suspect that I must have reached it at about the time when actual bombing was taking place in Spain. I could hardly have known then that one day I would be bombed myself, but my anxiety was strong enough to persuade Great-Aunt Agnes to tear out the offending page. It was too late. I dug my heels in more firmly than before and the lessons came to an end.

Another failure was in the field of art. I don't believe that my parents had any appreciation of painting at all. My father brought home from his travels a variety of peasant work to decorate his home, but the only picture which I remember on the walls was a print of Bellini's Doge. In the hall, however, was propped a large oil painting. It was almost impossible to see what the subject was under its layer of dark varnish and there was a three-cornered tear in one corner. So unbeautiful was this object that I could only assume that it must be valuable -- but if my stepmother, who eventually inherited all the contents of the house, ever made her fortune from it, she has kept the matter secret.

Frequently, though, I was taken to the National Gallery so that I should know what great art looked like. These educational visits made me familiar with the regular collection but brought little pleasure. The pictures seemed dark and uninteresting and I found unpleasant the sloppy Madonnas and outsize babies which particularly appealed to my mother.

When I was twenty-one, on my first visit to Paris, I wandered into the Jeu de Paume and found myself in an exhibition of Impressionist paintings. Their light and colour and vigour literally took my breath away and I sat there, dizzy with pleasure, for several hours. Nobody had ever told me that such work existed. So perhaps my early art education had not been a failure after all: for its limitations allowed me the excitement of discovering a new world all by myself.

That excitement encouraged me to read about the lives and struggles of some of the painters I newly admired, and as a consequence I became a firm believer in the importance of buying painters from living artists rather than dead Old Masters. I like to think of my cheques being used to buy food and clothing and holidays -- and the greatest pleasure of all has been actually to commission a painting or a piece of sculpture.

If my parents lacked enthusiasm for painting, they made up for it with music. Neither of them had any musical training, but they must have had -- and passed on -- a natural love for music. It can hardly be accidental that their ten grandchildren include a piano teacher, an opera company's répétiteur and an Oxford organ scholar as well as school and university orchestral players on the violin, cello, trombone, oboe and French horn.

Both my parents liked to sing. The high point of my father's otherwise grim years in the army came shortly after the end of the Great War when the

Paris Opera put on a gala performance of Faust but found itself short of able-bodied men for the chorus. He was recruited to make up the numbers, and for ever afterwards, when pressed into washing up after Sunday lunch, would enliven the chore with a vigorous rendering of *E'en the bravest heart must swell* or some other Faustian gem. There was even a sense in which music could be said to have started off my father's career as a published writer, for it was soon after his marriage that he joined a concert-party group to perform 'humorous songs' -- a pot-pourri of familiar tunes to which he had written new words; these were printed as sheet music.

My mother did not join in the vigorous singing of the washing-up squad. Her voice was sweet and true and she could accompany herself on the baby grand piano which was a surprising article of furniture to find in a house with little money for luxuries. She liked to sing hymns, and these are what I first remember learning myself. *Jesus bids us shine with a clear, pure light; like a little candle burning in the night* was a typical example. Do small children still, I wonder, earnestly trill such sentiments?

It may have been this early start which has always caused me to regard hymn singing as something quite separate from worship. When, nowadays, I am forced into a church by the claims of a wedding or funeral, I refuse to speak the creed, in which I have no belief, because that would be insincere, but will express the most preposterous sentiments in song, because somehow that doesn't count.

My first musical instruments were a pipe and a ukelele, but before long I began to have piano lessons from a teacher, Miss Haddon, who called once a week at the house. These continued for six or seven years, and by the end my chief delight was to earn praise for improvement after a week in which I had done no practice at all. 'Composing', with much crashing of chords, was always great fun; but sight-reading was a challenge rarely met, and my general impression is that I had not the slightest talent for the piano. Yet I still possess, rolled up with rather more impressive documents, certificates to prove that for several years I won first prize for my age in the Harrow Music Festival Competition. No doubt this only means that the other competitors were even less gifted. Although at the age of eleven I was sent up to London to be auditioned for a scholarship at Trinity College of Music, I didn't want it and didn't win it.

Eventually I grew tired of the piano, a cold instrument, and persuaded my parents to let me have violin lessons. They were a waste of money: I should have started years earlier. I had a good ear and could play in tune, but never mastered the mysterious art of vibrato. However, the violin did at least allow me the entrée, at the age of fifteen, to the Harrow County school orchestra.

It was an extremely poor orchestra -- as I realised when I later attended the impressive concerts in which my son and daughter played, at Winchester and St Paul's respectively --and its main task was to provide accompaniment at the annual carol concert. But the richer texture of orchestral playing was what I had been missing during my struggles with solo instruments and I was easily persuaded to fill a gap by borrowing the school viola and teaching myself to play it in lunch-hour practices.

Later I discovered an even more satisfactory instrument; almost a one-man band. I acquired first of all a club accordion and later a piano accordion: loud and cheerful, and useful for accompanying camp-fire sing-songs.

If all this instrumental experimentation had any long-term consequence, it was for my children rather than myself. For most musical instruments an early start is essential, and so they were condemned to piano practice just as I had been -- but with the promise that they could move to any other instrument as soon they felt strongly enough to choose. Each in turn took advantage of this offer: Jocelyn played the oboe and Jonathan the French horn. Each in turn abandoned their instruments, as I had done, at the age of eighteen. The exercise was a valuable one, all the same. The ability to read a score and to play -- to play almost anything -- is an important ingredient in the enjoyment of listening to music.

As well as struggling with these various musical instruments, I -- like my parents -- enjoyed singing, and longed to be a professional singer. My great-aunt possessed a gramophone with a huge, curved trumpet. She also owned complete sets of many of the D'Oyly Carte operas. To listen to a full performance was a lengthy business, because it was necessary to rewind the machine after each short (78 rpm) record, and continually to sharpen the needles. But we listened to the recordings over and over again, and I was allowed to choose which parts I would like to sing through. Like many a child before me, I used to indulge in day-dreams of the performance in which the star would be taken ill and an appeal would be made to the audience: 'Is there anyone here who is word- and note-perfect in the part?' I was about ten at the time.

It was never going to happen. Growing older, I realised that I had good pitch and could hold a part; and I could reach high notes. But compared to my sister Hilary, a magnificent contralto, my voice was pleasant rather than powerful: I had never been taught to project it and knew in my heart that I would never be a soloist. All the same...

In spite of all my mother's endeavours, it was someone else who was to have a more important influence on my pleasure in music. The music mistress when I first arrived at Harrow County was a large and extrovert blonde. All the girls adored her, and when she left to get married any successor would have found it difficult to fill her shoes. Her actual successor, Miss Crowle, was young and diffident, with no experience of maintaining discipline. The music room, a wooden building set a little apart from the rest of the school, became a riot area as she endeavoured actually to teach some music theory instead of organising jolly sing-songs.

I was fifteen, and in the term after her arrival I became a junior prefect. Feeling sorry for the new teacher, I set myself the task of making sure that at least one class in the week would pay her some attention. She already knew me as a member of the junior choir and the orchestra. Now perhaps she was grateful, and it was in her power to offer a reward.

Miss Crowle was a member of the London Bach Choir and a friend of its conductor, Dr Reginald Jacques. The choir was about to start rehearsals for Bach's St Matthew Passion and for much of the work would need to be divided into eight parts rather than the usual four. In two places during the performance a ninth group was required, to sing the 'ripieno' above the rest. It was traditional to bring in a few extra singers for this part. Miss Crowle was invited to train a small group. Most of those she chose were sixth-formers; but she added my name to the list.

The arrangement was that we should practise our two choruses with her in the schoolroom, needing to join the full choir only for the first and last rehearsals before the performance. But that first rehearsal swept me off my feet. So many singers, filling the air with such magnificent music! I had a pass to admit me to rehearsal as though I were a proper member of the choir, and I used it as often as I could, learning the soprano parts of all the choruses and not merely the ripieno lines. When the time came for the performance in the Royal Albert Hall, there was one more soprano in the choir than Dr Jacques knew about. My fellow-schoolgirls looked at me disapprovingly as I sang my head off. It was the start of a hobby which was to give me many years of intense pleasure -- and which directly inspired the first book of mine to be published: *Murder to Music*.

Since that first performance I have sung in a variety of venues. The

Oxford Bach Choir rehearsed, when I was an undergraduate, in the gallery of the university museum, sending the sound swirling round the skeletons of dinosaurs, and gave its concerts in the uncomfortable grandeur of the Sheldonian theatre. I have practised in parish halls and sung in churches, some heavy with dust and others stifling with incense. I've sung in the still air of the Egyptian desert and in Hyde Park, with aeroplanes triumphantly flying past overhead on some patriotic wartime occasion. Less surprisingly I've sung in cathedrals where the music lingered in transepts or behind pillars.

In a boys' prep school I've acted as 'stuffing', sitting out of sight on a low bench and letting the boy sopranos have their heads on the bits they knew but making sure that at least one person came in on the difficult leads. As secretary of Hampstead Choral Society I organised concerts in the Royal Festival Hall, where the acoustics in its early years made each member of even the largest choir feel as though she were singing a solo; and as a penniless undergraduate I worked my way through a residential choral course by washing up, so that now I can never listen to a performance of 'Rio Grande' without remembering that Yorkshire folk require refreshment six times a day.

Singing hasn't proved to be a lifelong hobby. Little by little, as I grew older, my top notes disappeared, and by now I've become one of those who perpetually grumble about the way in which organists pitch hymns and carols too high. But it was good while it lasted -- and I still appreciate its legacy every time I listen to a recording or go to a concert. Works which have been studied and sung provide a deeper satisfaction than those which have merely been heard.

For all these happy experiences, both active and passive, I give thanks to Miss Jean Crowle, who helped me to discover that choral singing, in oratorio, was my kind of music.

Chapel and church

When our elder child, Jocelyn, was three years old I decided that the time had come for her to go to Sunday School. Since by that time I no longer called myself a Christian, I had not attended any of the churches in the area of Teddington, to which we had moved eighteen months earlier. I set out to explore, and after several Sunday mornings of sampling decided on a sect which called itself Reformed Anglican. There was something faintly heretical about its background, since all its priests appeared to have been ordained by or through a single Canadian bishop who had cut himself off from mainstream orthodoxy. But I liked the hearty -- almost non-comformist -- way in which the congregation sang the hymns, and Jocelyn was duly enrolled. (She gave it three months before complaining that she was tired of colouring pictures and having to keep inside the lines; and that was the end of my attempt at religious education.)

Jeremy watched this lengthy process with incredulous amusement, unable to understand why I should set such store by Sunday School. I had to sit down and think of some reason that would hold more water than maternal instinct: and it didn't take much thought. Until I was eleven years old, church life and social life were the same thing. I made no friends either in the rough and tumble of Greenhill Elementary School or amongst the posh private school girls who lived in our street. All my friends were Baptists. Disregarding the matter of denomination, I must have thought that Jocelyn too would have a friendless childhood unless she was accepted into a church community. She knew better.

Both my parents were Baptists and both were teetotallers. In each respect my mother was the more fervent. With one small exception, neither spirits, wine nor beer ever entered the house. Her terror of drunken men and the vehemence with which she denounced the evil of even a single sip of the forbidden liquids might well have tempted me to overdo my new freedoms after I left home. But it didn't; and it may be that I enjoy drinking wine with my meals all the more for having had a completely watery upbringing. Unlike my sister Hilary, who was pressurised into signing the pledge when she was only ten or eleven years old, I never promised to remain a total abstainer for ever, and so was spared the guilt of breaking a vow.

The exception to this domestic prohibition was a tiny bottle of what was referred to as medicinal brandy, which was kept in the bathroom. On one occasion, which I think must have been near the time of my third mastoid operation, I was given a spoonful of this. I really must have been very ill indeed for my mother to have opened the bottle. Ever since that day I have associated brandy with pain and have never been able to enjoy it.

My mother's abhorrence of the demon drink was such that, had she been well enough to come to my wedding, it might well have been an occasion celebrated only with fizzy lemonade. This could have set the relationship between the two families off to a bad start, for Jeremy's father was a brewer and his only other son had already married the daughter of a teetotal Methodist minister. Fortunately, although not drinking himself, my father was happy to order the expected champagne for that day.

His own reason for abstinence was because he had never found anything that he liked better than Tizer. As a young man fighting in the Great War he was wounded in the mouth and throat; and when his comrades poured down rum to revive him it started an association between pain and alcohol which was far stronger than my own aversion to brandy and which never left him.

In doctrine, too, my mother -- a minister's daughter --allowed no compromise. She was a fundamentalist. Everything in the Bible was true -- so it was easy to distress her as I grew older and was able to indulge in the parent-baiting sport of text quotation. I doubt whether my father felt as strongly on the matter, but it was not worth his while to argue. He too went regularly to church until the war disrupted his steady civil servant's timetable. It was not just my own social life which was bound up with the College Road Baptist Church, but that of the whole family.

It was a thriving community. In other areas it would have been called chapel: but in Harrow for some reason it was church. Its activities were by no means confined to Sundays. It owned its own tennis club, at which my parents played. It had a strong amateur dramatic society: my father was one of the stars, and I was brought in if a female child was needed. The only production which I remember in any detail was The Farmer's Wife: but there were many more than that. There was a debating club -- my father shone in that, as well -- and lecture evenings through the winter. Naturally there was a choir, which needed to practise as well as to sing in services; and a Young Wives' Circle. For me there were Brownies and Guides and, later on, a youth club.

In addition, special events were organised. Once a year three double-decker buses would draw up outside the church and take all the children who had attended Sunday School regularly off to Ashridge for a picnic and impromptu sports day. At least twice a year came Sales of Work: they sound humdrum, but I remember them as exciting events, when a penny or two might buy a satisfactory Christmas present to be given away. There was certainly a Christmas party; and a concert, which was more of an ordeal since everyone was expected to perform a party piece.

More to be taken for granted was the Beginners' Sunday School, for which the under-fives were shepherded out of the morning service before the sermon began in order to enjoy their own story. This was a necessary precaution, since Mr Rendall's sermons were none of your ten-minute Anglican affairs but could, if the spirit was on him, continue for more than half an hour.

Older children were expected to sit quietly through the sermon, although it was permitted to read the hymnbook or the missionary magazine. For them there was a proper Sunday School from two to four in the afternoon; and after the age of about fourteen they would be expected to return for the evening service as well. Now that it no longer plays any part at all in my life, I find it extraordinary to look back on such activity: but perhaps it is all going on as strongly as ever: it is from my own choice that I feel no wish to be involved. It was hardly surprising, though, that at the time I should feel myself well provided with company and activities in this single community, and only began to look outside it when I went to Harrow County School and found congenial schoolfriends for the first time.

Nor is it surprising that as a result of this upbringing I should -- very briefly -- have felt it my duty to offer my children similar opportunities. I can't, however, have expected that an early inoculation of religion would 'take', for the consequence of my own total immersion was predictable. At the age of about sixteen everybody rebels against something, and I was no exception.

It was music which first drew me outside. I enjoyed the hearty hymn-singing of the Baptists, but I also liked listening to the choral services in the local Anglican church. I became a regular attender at evensong.

This did not go unnoticed. The minister's wife made it clear that a Baptist Sunday School teacher -- for by now I had attained that degree of seniority -- could not be allowed to play truant and consort with the enemy. Naturally, my response was to abandon my class. I needed the time for homework, anyway.

Mrs Rendall turned her guns against my mother instead, and they had the kind of quarrel which only a storm in a teacup can justify. My own feeble sixteen-year-old argument was predictable: that there was only one God and the name of the building in which He was worshipped was immaterial. This was brushed aside by both parties, and it did not take me long to realise that the row was about something completely different.

Many years earlier my mother had organised yet another grouping within the community. There were already Bible groups for every age and taste -- except one. She started a Sunday afternoon meeting for servants.

In the thirties many suburban families, even on quite low incomes, kept one young maidservant to scrub floors and serve tea. We had enjoyed this privilege ourselves for a few months, offering shelter to an unfortunate girl who had been hastily dismissed by her previous employer when she was found to be pregnant -- but even my mother's generous heart did not extend to keeping her after the baby was born. Although money was certainly short, I suspect that my mother in any case disliked the idea of being an employer. She would always have felt too sorry for the girl, shivering in the unheated attic, to be able to criticise poor work.

It is perhaps because I grew up in a household without servants that I am no more willing than she was to be an employer, although for a different reason. I appreciated help while the two children were very young, but have done without it ever since they started school because I like to have the house to myself while I'm writing. The need to chat to a daily help over a mid-morning coffee has always seemed too high a price to pay for a clean house. I suppose that what I have inherited is the inability to ignore someone who is working for me; but many employers sixty years ago did not find this a problem.

Unlike the servants in large establishments, suburban maids often led lonely lives. They were unable to go to church on Sunday mornings because they were preparing Sunday lunch, but they did as a rule have the afternoon free. Under my mother's auspices they were given somewhere to congregate for what was a social as much as a religious occasion, followed by tea.

These teas had been amongst the highlights of my young life. The Bible study group and Sunday School both ended at four o'clock, so that because of my mother's leadership I was able to join in the spread. Each of the maids brought a cake -- no doubt made with her mistress's ingredients -- and friendly rivalry turned the meal into a feast. My own regular favourite was a sponge cake rich with jam and cream. The fact that it took me several years to discover that this one was not home-made, but bought from Lyons, is a tribute to the fact that no shop cakes ever entered my own home.

Whether from snobbery or jealousy, the minister's wife did not approve of the maids' group and may have been resenting their affection for my mother for many years. The meetings had lapsed when my mother went to the country at the beginning of the war, and the proposal that they should be started again when she returned to Harrow met with strong opposition. Although I was the ostensible cause of what became a bitter argument, it was not really about my defection at all. For once I was wholly on my mother's side. The Baptist Church had been, after her family, almost her whole life; it came as a blow to find that she had such a powerful enemy within it. I sympathised with her distress; but that did not prevent me from making matters worse as I resolved never to become involved in such a way myself.

Taking the opportunity to transfer myself entirely to the Church of England -- because a girl with my upbringing needed a little longer to absorb the possibility that there was such a thing as life without any denominational label at all -- I found myself a heathen: past the age at which an Anglican would have been confirmed, but not yet arrived at that for the Baptist service of adult baptism. This seemed of little importance -- until some years later, as the time of my marriage approached. Since I had never even been baptised, I was not eligible to marry in church.

Hastily -- since I was perfectly willing to become an official Anglican, but had simply never got round to doing anything about it -- the necessary ceremony was arranged. Jeremy, my future husband, agreed to be my godfather, and it was the vicar of his parish who prepared me. These sessions were the cause of grave doubts. Although I had never shared my mother's belief in the truth of every word of the Bible, it did seem to me that I ought to believe what I was about to promise to believe: and when I read the Thirty-Nine Articles for the first time I had to confess that I couldn't possibly take them all on board.

'Don't worry about that,' said the vicar cheerfully. 'None of us believe all of them either.'

I went along with his easy-going attitude and duly became my fiancé's god-daughter, but it bothered me all the same; and in a sense the moment when I officially became a member of the Church of England was the moment when I ceased to respect it. The more important moment which decided me that I could live not only without a denominational doctrine but also without God came later: a badly-briefed chaplain in a maternity hospital spent too long trying to persuade me that God was solely responsible for giving me a beautiful baby -- and then had some difficulty in trying to explain why He should have presented me with one which had been born dead.

Extricating oneself from a strongly religious childhood can never be easy. Some people undoubtedly over-react. Others may never wish to escape, and as long as no doubts ever creep in, perhaps they are the fortunate ones. My mother compensated for the unhappiness of her later life by concentrating on the coming pleasures of Heaven. I prefer to work at this life on the assumption that it is all I have. I have been very lucky and very happy: but I give the credit for that to my family and my work. In other words, I have escaped.

Family at war

The term 'adolescent' was not widely used during the nineteen-forties, and the teenager had not yet been invented. Children were children until they left school.

This form of words came very near to reflecting a true state of affairs. Physical maturity arrived later then than it does now; and a single-sex school which inflicted several hours of homework each evening, combined with the fact that it was often dangerous to be out after dark, acted as an effective check on emotional maturing. Nevertheless, all the turbulent emotions of the teenager were in place, even if no one had a word for them.

The beginning of the war affected schoolgirls in ways which differed according to their ages, almost by the month. Sixth formers who went straight into the women's services often discovered administrative skills in themselves which might have lain dormant for ever in marriage. Girls of fifteen and sixteen grew up to enjoy the often bitter-sweet romances of a *carpe diem* society: behind the black-out of London life there was a good deal of gaiety. Younger children had to do what they were told and were ushered uncomprehendingly into shelters or on to evacuation trains.

At the age of thirteen when the war started, I belonged to none of these categories. I had not previously been a rebellious child, and I did not become one overnight. My school closed down and my father very reasonably decided that his children should be sent to stay with his mother rather than be evacuated to strangers. Hilary and Lauriston were aged seven and three, so naturally our mother came with us. I don't remember protesting immediately. We were used to spending holidays at Ibstock. This one would be longer than usual, that was all. My sisters could attend the village school, while for me there was a grammar school at nearby Coalville.

I walked over to inspect it. It was not as close as all that, and the walk would not be much fun on dark winter nights. Blackout restrictions had already been imposed, but in the country there were few street lamps to start with. I returned to my grandmother's house in a sulk. The school building, I announced, was hideous: a mass of bright red brick. I may not have wanted to confess in front of my grandmother, who spoke in a Leicestershire accent and dropped or added aitches in an unusual pattern, that I couldn't imagine myself ever making friends with children who seemed to be speaking a different language, and it was immediately clear that they would mock my own 'standard' accent.

After brooding for about a week I announced my decision. I proposed to return to Harrow. Although my own school was closed, Pinner County School was outside the evacuation zone and could be reached by bus. I could look after myself in the house perfectly well.

This last statement was nonsense, of course, but I believed it with such fervour that -- to my own astonishment when I look back on it -- I won the ensuing battle. It helped, no doubt, that the first wailing of an air raid siren which accompanied Neville Chamberlain's announcement of war had not proved in fact to be the precursor of the expected raids. But my mother was extremely anxious as she accompanied me home and set about making arrangements for a permanent split in the family. My father, who over the previous ten years had become in his spare time a great success on Foyle's lecture circuit, was about to be transferred from the Office of Works to the Ministry of Information and would be away from home a great deal, delivering propaganda lectures. It was arranged that two elderly ladies, anxious to move from their home in central London, should live in the house to be company: I was never absolutely clear whether they were looking after me or I was looking after them.

I ought to be thoroughly ashamed of the stresses I placed on my mother both at this time and later. She did her best to divide her time between the two houses during the next few years. I find it interesting that my surviving sister, Laurie, and I each remember her as being more often away with the other. I suppose my own clearest memories are of the periods when I felt independent, free of family life. Laurie, ten years younger, would also be most aware of the times when her mother was not with her, although for the opposite reason, of unhappiness. She dealt with this by transferring her love to her grandmother.

This was yet another blow to my mother, who was in a no-win situation. She sincerely felt that her place was with her two younger children, in spite of finding life in her mother-in-law's house uncongenial as a long-term arrangement. This was not simply a matter of Hilary and Lauriston's ages, although that must have been the main reason. My grandmother was kind but she was not in any sense cultured, and the village school was unlikely to provide much intellectual stimulus. Its most obvious achievements in Laurie's case were to give her a thick Leicestershire accent and ringworm. For several years she wore a succession of pixie bonnets because badly-regulated treatment had left her bald.

A mother who had once been a teacher would have been strongly aware of the need to oversee her children's education. She was frightened about the prospect of being bombed, and this fear too must have strengthened her inclination to stay in Ibstock. Yet as long as she remained there, she felt enormous guilt about not being with me -- even though I was the one who had made this impossible. So great was my selfishness at the time that I was not prepared even to recognise that a problem existed.

The consequence of this teenage rebellion is quite straightforward. Had I spent the five years from the age of thirteen to seventeen at Coalville Grammar School I should be a completely different person now. The importance of my revolt is that I realised that at the time. The ship of my life was veering off course, and I needed to get my own hand on the tiller.

Meanwhile the headmistress of Harrow County had been conducting her own rebellion. The expected bombs had not yet started to fall and not all her pupils had left the area. Air raid shelters were dug underneath the playing fields, windows were criss-crossed with brown sticky tape, and the school reopened.

When the bombing finally started, Harrow had its full share of alerts. It suffered nothing like the intensity of destruction in the City and dock areas and quite possibly most of the damage done was accidental. At the time, however, we were conscious that both the main railway routes to the north ran through the suburb; as a small child my favourite walks used to be to the bridges from which I could watch the Royal Scot or the Flying Scotsman speeding romantically northwards. In addition, there was a large railway junction not far away from my home. We probably gave the Luftwaffe credit for more meticulous targeting than was possible at that time in assuming that it was deliberately attacking local communications.

During almost six years of war our quiet suburb experienced various kinds of air attack. The V2 rockets which arrived at the very end of the period did enormous damage, but approached so silently that there was no point in feeling frightened of them. The V1 flying bombs -- popularly known as doodle-bugs -- which preceded them worked on the opposite principle. Their rasping approach could be heard from a considerable distance, and everyone in the street or playground would freeze, listening for the sinister moment when the engine would cut out. It was the silence which was dangerous, for then the bomb was gliding towards the ground. But although our house was to suffer from one of these eventually, they did not cause personal fear any more than the rockets did: if you could still hear a doodle-bug overhead, you knew with relief that it was going somewhere else. The anxiety lay in assessing the direction of the silent glide and wondering whether it was making for your home, your friends, your family.

Incendiary bombs were the only kind with which schoolgirls might be expected to deal. From the age of sixteen we took our turns at firewatching on the school roof and discovered previously unknown pleasure in stars and sunrises. We were equipped with stirrup pumps and buckets of water and sand, which dealt well enough with the specimen provided by the fire service as part of our training, but might not have had much effect in controlling a mass attack.

As I watch television news programmes nowadays which graphically illustrate the relentless twenty-four-hour bombardment of unfortunate victims, I realise how surprising -- and fortunate -- it was that in my own years of being bombed the planes came either by night or by day: rarely both in the same period. There was one long spell in which wailing air raid sirens gave the alert regularly at nine in the morning, just after we had arrived at school, and did not announce the all clear until five. So, with gas masks and packed lunches in cardboard boxes slung over our shoulders, we spent the whole day in long narrow shelters: trenches cut into the ground and covered with earth. It can't have been good for either our health or our education; but even those damp days never made me wish that I had settled for Coalville Grammar School.

No doubt all these later attacks were made more easily bearable by the fact that they had been preceded by the blitz. The autumn and winter of 1940 ought to have given even the most pig-headed fourteen-year-old cause to consider that Leicestershire was a safer place to be. During the 'phoney war' my mother had divided her time between Ibstock and Harrow. As fear of a German invasion grew after the collapse of France, she was yet again trying to persuade me to come to the country, and so was at home -- her own home -- when the heavy raids began in September 1940.

The shelter arrangements at 3 Gerard Road were of dubious effectiveness. As war approached my father had arranged for a trapdoor to be cut in the floor of the breakfast room. Through this we could jump down into the foundations of the house, which were about four feet deep. Another opening had been cut through the rockery at the back of the house, to act as an escape route if the building collapsed on top of the trap door. An electric cable was fixed to the joists beneath the floor boards, with a single light bulb dangling from it, and camp beds and torches were taken down as soon as the need arose.

The snags were quick to show themselves. The space beneath the house was not a proper cellar, but merely a space. No attempt had been made to provide protection against blast by any kind of reinforcement. The ground, being of earth, was dirty and damp, the lack of height was claustrophobic and the single light which swayed with the vibration of bombs and guns made reading impossible as soon as a raid started. We did not possess any wireless set small enough to be moved between house and basement. There was nothing to do but lie and listen. It was in these dismal surroundings that I had one of the most important experiences of my life.

It was one of the bad nights. Although I never had to endure anything like the bombing of the East End, I was not interested in comparisons as the earth trembled and the air shuddered with noise. Much of the noise was made by anti-aircraft guns, but that was not much comfort. Both my parents were down below with me that night and they had been talking -- not to me, but for my benefit, as though the situation were perfectly normal. Gradually, though, they fell silent, and the vibrations of fear were added to the quaking atmosphere. My father was a stoical man, but my mother was easily frightened at the best of times, and she was finding this the worst of times.

Another plane passed overhead: another stick of bombs began to fall, screaming, towards the ground. A good deal of unscientific myth was developed in playground gossip: it was the fifth in a row which was the dangerous bomb; after that you were all right. As usual I began to count. On this occasion it was number four which fell close at hand. The blast temporarily deafened me, but I was not conscious of that at first. I was too busy staring at what was in front of my eyes.

The foundations of the house were columns of brick. From my camp bed I could see two of them and, as I watched, they bent into a curve. It seemed to happen very slowly and perhaps I only imagined the feeling that the ceiling -- the floor of the house -- was pressing down towards my head. What was certainly not imagination, though, was that if those columns arched out for even another millionth of an inch the curve would explode and the whole weight of the house would collapse on top of us. My mother screamed. I was frightened as well, but in my case fear brought silence. I shut my eyes. It seemed certain that in a few seconds I would be dead.

When I opened my eyes, the columns were straight again. The house, as we discovered later, had been damaged but was still standing. The raid continued for an hour or two, but at last the guns fell silent and we went to sleep.

The immediate consequence of this experience was that I refused ever to go down into the foundations again. The raids continued every night, but I had decided that I would rather be killed in my own bedroom than run the risk of being buried alive. When the sirens went I heard my mother calling me down, but pretended to be asleep -- even when she shook me by the shoulders and knew that I was defying her. I was too big to be manhandled, so in the end she went down by herself. The only precaution I was prepared to take was to put a pillow over my head to prevent my face from being cut by flying glass. It was perhaps more fortunate for me than I deserved that when -- four years later -- a flying bomb landed close enough to shatter or blow out every window in the house, I was spending the night firewatching on the school roof.

My refusal to take sensible precautions was another example of extreme selfishness, because my mother must have been as terrified on my behalf as on her own. Had there been any justice in her world, I would have agreed to accompany her when she hurriedly returned to Ibstock. But my love affair with London had already begun and I took a twisted kind of pleasure in sharing, to a lesser degree, the city's torments. My refusal to budge after our first near miss succeeded in convincing her that she could not persuade me to be sensible; she went back to the country alone.

War wrecks family life in many ways. It was probably inevitable that there would be separations within my own family, but I know that I was responsible for the worst of them, and for inflicting on my mother the feeling that whatever she decided to do would be unsatisfactory. I was prepared to admit it, but not to apologise.

Meanwhile, as I lay upstairs in my own bed on other occasions and listened to bombs whistling down and exploding -- one, two, three, four, five, gone over -- I became aware of another consequence of the night when the foundations bowed. I was alert to danger, certainly, but I was no longer frightened. Indeed, it seemed to me that I would never be deeply frightened for my own safety again. I had learned the lesson that fear, which has its value when precautions ought to be taken or a rapid escape is needed, is a useless emotion in other circumstances. To fear possible suffering is a waste of time if the suffering does not in fact occur, and will not help endurance if it does. Fear of death is an even more pointless exercise, since death is certain to come.

It isn't always possible to control physical reactions. My stomach muscles tense as tightly as anyone else's when an aeroplane unexpectedly plunges downwards in a storm. But I shall always be grateful for the lesson that I learned at the age of fourteen. In five seconds or twenty years I shall be dead. Why spoil those seconds or years by worrying about what is bound to happen?

2

One episode which caused me great puzzlement was connected with the war but actually took place before it began. It was never explained to me why, when I was eleven or twelve, a Jewish family came to live in our house.

I'm not even sure that I knew at the time that they were Jewish. There were two Jewish girls in my class at school, envied by the rest of us because they were allowed so many special days of holiday, but that was the extent of my acquaintance. When Mrs Spielmann and her sister and son arrived, I was told that they were Austrian, but had no idea why they had not stayed in Austria. It might have been better if someone had appealed to my sympathy, because they took over my bedroom and I couldn't wait for them to leave. The sister, a university teacher from Vienna, did not in fact stay long, but the other two settled in as though for ever.

They were immensely fat; fat enough to seem disgusting. Both my parents were large, but I had never before seen anyone as shapeless as this. They seemed content just to sit, and I could not understand that either. Few people in England were aware at that time of what was happening to the Jews in Europe, so it was perhaps not surprising that nobody gave me the information which might have induced understanding. Only several years later did I begin to realise the state of shock in which they must have been living. In Vienna they had been prosperous, with servants, and now were destitute. They spoke no English to start with and I imagine -- though this I have never known -- that Mrs Spielmann's husband must have been taken off to a labour camp before she and Hans left Austria.

Although my parents gave them shelter, there may have been a certain lack of sympathy here as well. My mother had a soft heart: but she had once been diddled by a Jewish furrier in Poland who took her money for the fur she chose but wrapped up something quite different. She never quite forgave the race for that one example of cheating.

My father, meanwhile -- as I discovered from his papers after his death -- felt that he had been misled. The Home Office demanded that every refugee should be sponsored by someone personally prepared to undertake support. He had signed the necessary forms for this unknown family, but only after being given an unofficial assurance that Mrs Spielmann would in practice be financed by her sister and by a special refugee fund. This did not happen. The fund proved inadequate and the sister failed to find work and was interned as an enemy alien when the war started. There was not enough money to spare in our own household to pay for outside accommodation for the mother and son. So until the outbreak of hostilities brought the fear of being bombed and prompted them to take refuge in the country, there they sat in my bedroom. I was not pleased about this. Later on, when I learned the truth of the situation, a sense of shame made me sympathetic to the Jews.

Any war may have terrible consequences for those caught up in it. It takes lives and it changes lives in a way all the more devastating for being outside personal control. But there can be trivial consequences as well, and even after so long I am still reminded of some of these.

Not all are personal to me. There must be thousands of my generation who find it very difficult to throw anything at all away, lest it should one day come in useful in a time of shortage; who still carefully untie and store pieces of string, or collect large envelopes for re-use even though they can perfectly well afford to buy such things new. But my age at the start of the war meant that I had six very impressionable years to acquire such squirreling habits: years in which, with my mother often absent or ill, I was struggling to learn the art of housekeeping.

Thirteen was not a bad age at which to adapt to war, if that was to be necessary at all. I was too young to fight and my father was too old, and I had neither the experience nor the imagination to visualise what lay ahead. In fact, an ill-defined sense of danger provided the element of adventure which I had often felt to be missing from my life; and because I had not yet had time to become set in my ways I was not likely to pine for the good old days of peace.

One of the many trivialities which had an effect was discovered on the morning after I watched the foundations of the house quiver. The blast had cracked one of the chimneys, making it dangerous to use the back boiler in the breakfast room which heated the water. The damage was not sufficiently serious to warrant the use of scarce building labour for an immediate repair; so for several years the only way in which it was possible to have a bath was to heat water in saucepans and the wash boiler and carry it upstairs. Even though we obeyed the injunction to allow ourselves only five inches of water, the first instalments were cool before the last arrived. There was no pleasure in taking a bath -- so it is not surprising that one of my greatest daily pleasures ever since has been to lie in a deep, hot bath. Showers may suffice for cleanliness, but a bath is a luxury.

Food rationing began in 1940, and I proved to be an amenable member of the family. I had rebelled against milk as soon as I came out of hospital, and my mother considered tea to be a drink for adults. So I drank water at all meals, and liked it. By the time I reached an age when I might have expected to take tea, my mother was gratefully appropriating my ration as well as her own, and neither of us saw any need to change the system. As a result I never learned to like the taste, and even now drink tea only when politeness absolutely demands it.

Very much the same applies to butter. Because the weekly ration was tiny, I was encouraged to eat bread 'dry' and still dislike having it 'greasy'. Whenever a doctor suggests to me that I could lose weight by cutting milk and butter out of my diet I can only sigh hopelessly: they disappeared from it almost entirely years ago.

The sweet ration was a different matter. I liked sweets as much as any child and before the war would ponder long and earnestly whether to invest my weekly penny pocket-money in the four-ounces-a-penny range or go upmarket to two-ounces-a-penny -- but usually ended up with a tub of sherbet with a liquorice straw or a packet of pink-tipped sweet cigarettes. My father, however, who neither smoked nor drank, had a need for chocolate which the whole family recognised as an addiction. I was no more honest than any other child when it came to stealing food; but not only did I recognise that his chocolate store was sacrosanct: I allowed him to have my ration. I have made up for it since.

Generalising wildly from such present pleasures as hot baths and chocolate I conclude that many of the most appreciated small treats of adult life represent childhood wishes at last fulfilled. Into this category comes car ownership. Although petrol rationing would have restricted the use of a car if we had owned one, the war cannot be blamed for this particular deprivation. Neither of my parents ever learned to drive. Trains were used for holidays and visits to London and bicycles for shorter distances. There were plenty of local buses, but I could not usually afford the fares. I'm sure it was very healthy for me to walk and cycle everywhere; but it could seem a depressing waste of time when the long trek in the school holidays to see my best friend, who had no telephone, ended with the discovery that she was out. I longed to be a car-owner, and learned to drive as soon as I married.

Drawing support from one of the favourite literary heroines of my childhood, Pollyanna, I suspect that some lack of comfort in childhood makes contentment in adult life more easily achieved. In material as well as in emotional terms, my life has steadily improved in quality over the past fifty years. I can thank the war for that.

Thought for food

My best youthful food memory must be dated soon after the United States came into the war. My friend Joan and I, at the age of about sixteen, were on a cycling/youth hostelling holiday. Whilst toiling up a Wiltshire hill we heard the sound of a military convoy overtaking us and paused, glad of the rest, while the lorries went past. The last lorry was filled with black GIs. I doubt whether I had ever seen a black man at close quarters before, but what happened next filled me with prejudice -- favourable prejudice -- for life; for as we waved they tossed out two oranges for us to catch. Perhaps a degree of deprivation is almost worth while when such a small gesture can produce such warmth of gratitude. An orange! An orange *each*!

That kind of specific deprivation came only with the war, of course. In my first twelve years I could never complain about being hungry.

During those years fish and chip shops were the only 'takeaways' and the concept of convenience food or ready meals was either unheard-of or too expensive. Our larder contained no shop cakes and very few tins, until the coming of war and the points system of rationing made it essential to stock them. The only 'convenience' intruders that I can remember were Camp Coffee, a bottled essence of such appalling taste that it could only have been bought by someone who never drank coffee herself; and Bird's Custard Powder, which produced a yellow lumpy sauce unless made with more care than my mother usually afforded it. (A generation which buys custard, if at all, in tins as a convenient improvement on the powder, may need to be reminded that 'proper' custard was once upon a time made exceedingly slowly with eggs.)

Also missing from our larder was anything out of season. Do children nowadays realise that peas have seasons? We certainly did, for the frozen pea had not yet been invented, leaving several months of the year at the mercy of cabbage. Fruit was bottled or made into jam, but if we wanted fresh strawberries we had to wait until the fruit ripened in the last week of June. This had some advantages, for there is a lot to be said for an awareness of changing seasons; but it did impose limitations on our diet.

The first food of the day throughout my early childhood was porridge. Eating this was a compulsory body-building duty, not a treat. It was cooked all night on the lowest possible gas in the top of a double saucepan, from which it emerged in the morning thick and lumpy; even lumpier than the custard.

As time passed (and, perhaps more relevantly, as I was entrusted with the Saturday shopping) porridge was restricted to winter, and breakfast cereals appeared on the table; chosen for their appeal to a ten-year-old. The purchase of Force entitled me to wear a Sunny Jim badge; and I remember also that Rice Krispies were popular because fairy stories in modern dress were printed on the packet. (From much the same motive I insisted on buying Izal lavatory paper during the period when comic versions of nursery rhymes were interleaved through the roll: my habit of sitting on the lavatory and unrolling until I had collected all the pictures was not greatly appreciated by the rest of the family.)

After school, my last meal was tea, although sometimes I would be offered a chip or two from the supper which awaited my father's return from work at precisely ten to six. But my main meal was in the middle of the day. Like most children, I called it dinner; and, probably like most children, had to survive an awkward transitional period later in life when establishing the time of day involved in an invitation to dinner.

The big meal of the week, when all the family ate together, came straight after morning service on Sunday. While we were at church, the Wall's ice cream delivery man would have tricycled up to leave a vanilla block in the outside lavatory. Shopping on Sunday was sinful; but the ice cream was paid for in advance, on Saturday, so that made it all right. A joint of meat would have been roasting in the oven. My favourite was chicken, but that was expensive; a very rare treat indeed.

Before the war, and for a year or two after it began, I used to go home from school for my dinner; but when daylight air raids began this was no longer possible. To the gas mask box which everyone carried was added a lunch box and we each paid the school threepence a week towards the cost of providing water and glasses and sweeping up the crumbs: we ate in our own classrooms -- or, of course, in the air raid shelters.

By the time I reached the sixth form, all-day air raids had come to an end. Doodle-bugs were too scattered and rockets too silent for any warning to be useful. It was no longer essential to carry lunch around, so I was given an allowance of a shilling a day to spend as I liked. A British Restaurant had opened in Harrow, as in most other towns, and would provide, for example, stew, potato and cabbage followed by jam sponge and custard for that price; but my preferred menu came from Joe Lyons. Here I regularly bought a bread roll without butter, an ice cream soda and an individual fruit pie. The sweet pastry shell of the square pie was generously stuffed with fruit which could be sucked out after the first corner had been bitten off: very different from the mean scraping of jam to which it was later reduced. I considered this a very well-balanced diet.

Eating in a restaurant -- even one as basic and cafeteria-style as a British Restaurant -- was an experience which would not normally have come my way. A vivid pre-war memory is of accompanying my parents to the Trocadero, where for some reason they had been invited to lunch by the local MP, Sir Isadore Salmon. An hors d'oeuvre trolley appeared with dozens of little dishes which dangled from a drum-like contraption and very cleverly, in my young opinion, always kept level as the drum turned to reveal the next layer.

My mother, served first and assuming this to be the main course (since the concept of a 'starter' was unknown in our house), pointed to one dish after another of fishy bits and meaty bits and salad bits until her plate was loaded. As I prepared to do the same, Sir Isadore tactfully warned me that there were more and better things to come. He should have been tactful earlier: my mother was unable to conceal her humiliation, whilst I was startled to realise that even a grown-up could be caught out in the world outside home. Eating-out was simply not part of her life.

Nor, in the sense of entertaining, was eating-in. My mother rarely gave dinner parties and rarely attended them. Her friends were all Baptists, and they met so frequently at the various church clubs that there was no need for formal arrangements. Besides, as rationing bit, it became extremely difficult to provide an interesting meal for more than the family -- as I discovered for myself as a young married woman -- and in my parents' case there would be no wine or drinks of any kind to make the occasion go with a swing.

My father, because of his increasing success as a lecturer, ought to have become more at ease with strangers, but was surprisingly diffident. From time to time, when I was seventeen or eighteen, he would take me to parties so that he could have someone to talk to; but he was nervous about interrupting anyone's conversation or performing introductions. I had to accept the fact that I would absorb very little social education from my parents.

As my mother's health deteriorated I needed to undertake more in the way of cooking, although I had no talent for it and it would have needed someone with much more experience than I could boast to make a success of eggless cakes or meatless stews. My father's tastes were extremely simple. Fish was for cats and salads were for rabbits: his own menu was restricted to sausage and chips, steak and chips, chop and chips, egg and chips. Well, there was no problem about the chips! Luckily, by the time I was expected to cope, he was only at home for a day or two a fortnight.

My mother was easier to please, with bland dishes like macaroni cheese, and when my sisters returned from Ibstock they appeared to be happy with such stodgy specialities as toad in the hole and pancakes. I don't remember being expected very often to cook meat, which was too scarce and precious to be risked with an untrained cook; and if some of my fish pies produced raised eyebrows, it could well have been because whale and snoek are not very nice.

One of the problems about food in my childhood was that it didn't keep. We had no freezer and no refrigerator -- and no guarantee that even an ingredient straight from the shop was fresh. A good many years had to pass before I felt it safe to abandon the once-essential habit of breaking each egg for an omelette separately into a small bowl before adding it to the rest, in case it should prove to be bad.

Greengrocers dealt with the problem of disposing of rotten fruit by refusing to let the customer see, let alone touch, what was going into her bag. Milk and meat would not last long in summer. Our meat safe, fastened to a north wall, kept out flies but could not hold in freshness; there was a good deal of surreptitious wiping with vinegar to remove any smell before it went into the oven. The leisurely progress of the milkman's horse-drawn cart meant that the milk was often warm before it arrived, and the battle to stop it turning was unending. We had a pottery bottle holder which stood in water to keep it cool, and a square of muslin, fringed with beads which weighed down the edges, to protect the top. But in spite of every effort, one of our most regular -- though unpopular -- puddings was junket, made by adding rennet to warm milk just before it reached the stage of separating into curds and whey.

Although, when I look back on it, I probably had more experience in the kitchen than a good many seventeen-year-old schoolgirls, the immediate consequence of this regime was a well-justified lack of confidence in my ability to cook. University did nothing to improve the situation and my fiancé shared my doubts about his gastronomic future. It was at his suggestion that I went off to Edinburgh before we were married to do a

'Bride's course'. This taught me how to iron without electricity and when to hang my horsehair mattresses out of the window: two skills which have never been of much practical use, I'm glad to say. I also learned how to make almost anything with oatmeal; and forgot the lessons as quickly as possible.

Food was still rationed when Jeremy and I moved into our first home, and so a little time had to pass before I discarded the Edinburgh Book of Plain Cooking and instead began to consult the Penguin Cordon Bleu Cookery, the most useful birthday present he ever gave me. But the consequence of my earlier hours in the kitchen was clear enough in both stages, plain and fancy. I was brought up to take it for granted that food should be prepared at home, and that it was the woman who should prepare it. No doubt almost everyone of my age feels the same way; but we are a diminishing group.

Another of my children's friends -- not the young philosopher -- came to lunch one Sunday. The meal was unpretentious family food, but he gave me an odd look. 'You cook!' he said -- or perhaps, 'You cook?' It was not quite a statement, not quite a question; just an oddity noted.

I may not remain odd for much longer. The rot began to set in years ago when I made soup with my own glut of tomatoes and some expensive cream and realised after a lot of work that the result tasted exactly as though it had come from a tin. It began to spread at a faster rate when more recently I discovered that I could buy ready-made pâtés just as delicious as those I had laboriously prepared myself in the past, and it finally raged out of control when a guest, eating my home-made Coronation Chicken, remarked appreciatively that it must have come from Marks and Spencer. Consequences do not necessarily have to endure for ever.

Making and mending

There were no all-purpose clothes in my childhood. I had school clothes, Brownie uniform, Saturday-and-holiday clothes and Sunday best.

The concept of 'best clothes' seems almost to have disappeared in ordinary life now, when everyone who has dressed neatly for work all week chooses to spend the whole weekend in casual -- often sporting -- wear. But at least until I was thirteen I took it for granted that before leaving for church every Sunday morning I would put on a neat dress and an overcoat -- usually dark blue, with velvet lapels -- and matching hat. Because I was the eldest of three girls, overcoats started new with me, and were handed down later. (The handing-down system worked less to my advantage when applied to books, which were appropriated when I was thought to have grown out of them and never returned, even when I would have preferred to keep them.)

Dressing in this demure manner imposed demure behaviour. The three little Newman girls made, I feel sure, a pretty picture on their sedate way to church.

Saturdays were a different matter. On Saturdays alone I had some say in the matter of appearance, and almost invariably chose to wear khaki shorts, in which I could pretend I was a boy. They were ideal for cycling, climbing trees and scrambling out of the attic window on to the top of the roof, to the dismay of any neighbours who caught sight of me.

School clothes changed their nature when I was eleven. There was no uniform at Greenhill Elementary: a hand-knitted jersey over a flannel skirt was usual wear. But once I was accepted for Harrow County, a major shopping expedition became necessary. I needed a navy blue mackintosh, navy blazer with badge, navy felt hat with hatband, navy gloves (to be worn at all times in the street when in school uniform) and navy V-necked sweater with pink and brown edging stripes to match the hatband.

All this was outerwear and standard for the time, but the part of the uniform to be worn in class was unusually horrid. There was a long-sleeved white blouse with a square neck. No doubt this needed to be washed less often than a style with a collar, but since most children are short on neck the effect was unbecoming. Over this went a gym slip with a square yoke, from which fell inverted pleats. Permanent pleating had not then been invented, and to have stitched in the edges would probably have been regarded as cheating. Every time the garment needed pressing, which was often, the pleats had to be sewn in place first.

Even when new, this was an inelegant garment, and the effect was not enhanced by the tightness with which we all tied our narrow sashes (navy for the rank and file, pink and brown for prefects and members of school teams) in the effort to pretend that we possessed waists). For a girl with my figure, the 'sack-of-potatoes' taunt was well justified. I longed for summer, when for about six weeks a blue summer dress was approved.

Even in summer, though, black stockings were still to be worn, ridiculous though they looked with a light dress. Black stockings have come into fashion, even junior fashion, in recent years, but in the nineteen-thirties they were worn only under compulsion, and almost exclusively by servants and schoolchildren. Suspended from liberty bodices or gently sagging from garters, they were made of wool or lisle and required almost weekly darning, so that heel blisters were a permanent complaint for most of us. Only half way through the war, when clothes rationing began to bite, did common sense prevail and white socks became permitted wear.

There was no concession in the matter of shoes, though: black lace-ups in the street and ward shoes inside the school. Ward shoes (named, I suppose, after hospital wear, although that explanation did not occur to me at the time) were also black and low-heeled, but with a strap. Every morning and lunch-hour break involved shoe-changing, for to wear outdoor shoes indoors was one of the greatest school crimes.

Some measure of relief came on reaching the sixth form, when seniority could be marked by the wearing of a navy-blue skirt with white blouse and striped tie. At last it was possible to look like a normal human being.

Except for gym (before it was rechristened as PE). Someone had had the bright idea that we should be taught to sew in our first year by making something useful; and the something was a garment in which to do gym and play games. (While it was in the making, we exercised in our white blouses and navy blue knickers.) With immense care but frequent unpicking of stitches we sewed two pieces of soft blue material together to create a short sleeveless shapeless garment with round neck and elasticated waist: the bottom two inches of the side were split to allow free movement. I imagine that the effect was derived from Isadora Duncan. The memory of this and of the gym slip enable me to say confidently that Harrow County School did little to develop any dress sense in its pupils.

The war posed a particular problem for my generation: our bodies started to develop just as clothes rationing came in. There were special concessions for children; but even so, any coupons not swallowed by the demands of school uniform were needed for articles such as shoes and stockings which could not be made at home. For the rest, a good deal of ingenuity was exercised. Whether by accident or because she had guessed that the problem would arise, my mother had laid in a stock of Harris tweed and Liberty voile. One result was that I wore the same material for my 'best' summer dress for about five years, in different styles: but it was a pretty blue flowered pattern and I didn't mind.

When private stocks ran out, my mother sacrificed some of her own old dresses to be cut up for us, replacing them by using furnishing fabrics for herself: these were not on coupons. A useful source of underwear was parachute silk, from parachutes which had presumably been found faulty. We all grew adept at designing petticoats and nightdresses in a way which would best make use of the narrow triangles into which the fabric was divided; and embroidery, which was dull as a school subject, made the finished articles look positively shop-like. Later in the war parachutes of nylon were available as well, although these were more difficult to handle. Anything useful was snatched up and hoarded for emergency use later. At least fifteen years after the war ended I found a box in which I had kept the last parachute and the last length of Harris tweed, just in case. By then I lived in a centrally heated house and the tweed was unbearably heavy for indoor wear.

More ingenuity was required for special events. There was not much call for evening dress during wartime suburban life, and my mother had a sufficient stock of clothes for herself. But I had to acquire a first long dress from scratch, and it seemed extravagant to waste coupons on a garment which might only be worn once or twice a year. However, I had a bright cotton housecoat (i.e.dressing gown) which I thought very pretty, and spent hours edging the neck, cuffs, waist and hem with black velvet ribbon in order to transform it. It could always return to housecoat use between dances.

All this might have put me off dressmaking for good; but in fact I enjoyed the need to be adventurous and found it ridiculously easy to make clothes for myself and my daughter later on, when material could simply be bought in shops and the use of a paper pattern no longer resembled doing a jigsaw puzzle. I might have been better dressed, of course, if I had made less and bought more; but as with writing books, the pleasure was in the making.

Except for one pleasure -- a pleasure shared by many young women towards the end of the war. Some of them behaved shamelessly to acquire a first pair of nylon stockings. I was too young to be flirtatious, and all I had to do was to wait for my father to come home from the United States. He had been lecturing there on behalf of the Ministry of Information; and because he was a salaried civil servant, he could not accept any fees. But kind people pressed gifts on him. My first lipstick was a present from Max Factor -- although my father hoped mildly, as he handed it over, that I would wait a few years before using it. From Walt Disney I received a signed original animation painting used in *Bambi*. And from someone unknown in New York came my first pair of nylons.

They were very shiny, very sheer, and very very very strong. I kept them for seven years. Admittedly, they were worn only for special events, and not for scrambling through prickly hedges. But it did seem to me that they had been created to be indestructible. As I struggled to preserve later and lesser pairs of nylons, mending ladders of almost invisible rungs with a gadget like a crochet hook, it seemed clear that the inventor of nylon had meant his product to last; it was a pity that mean-minded manufacturers, needing repeat orders, had converted a pair of nylons into yet another disposable object. Still, at least I have never as an adult had to spend my evenings darning black woollen stockings.

There is no resemblance at all between my adolescent attitude to clothes and those of youngsters today. The idea of begging parents to provide a particular brand of shoe or pair of jeans so that I could look the same as anyone else in my free time would have been quite alien to me. When so much of my life was spent in uniform -- for school, for Guides, and even in a sense for church -- my only wish for the rest of the time was to look different from everyone else. But the details of the difference were largely a matter of chance: what materials were to hand and what could be done with them. It was sufficient of a triumph to possess a garment which was suitable for its purpose, without asking myself whether it conformed to anyone's current rules.

If 'fashion', in the sense of changing styles, existed during the war, I didn't know about it. It's true that when Dior's New Look burst on to the scene in 1947 I dashed as enthusiastically as every other young woman to spend my precious coupons on at least one garment with its flatteringly pinched waist and long, wide, swirling skirt: but that was a gesture of liberation from all the years of shortages and skimpy utility standards rather than a fashion statement. It was the only exception to my dislike of dressing in the same way as everyone else.

In the following years, when change for change's sake became the order of the day, I resented the bullying of the fashion industry, growling under my breath when I found that this year's mackintosh would not cover last year's skirt. After living for so many years in London, where women really did seem to care about skirt lengths and 'in' colours, it came as a relief to find that in Oxford, where I live now, very few people take the slightest notice of such things. When fashion imposes a uniform, someone like myself, brought up in uniform, prefers to look the other way.

The play's the thing!

Although television was invented before the war, I had never heard of it. It was wireless which provided domestic entertainment, and there were plenty of grumblers to say then, as their descendants say now, that family life and the art of conversation were being killed by this intrusion.

Although my first wireless memories are of Children's Hour -- and in particular of the Toytown plays -- my impression later on was that programmes were a pleasant way of drawing the family together. This was particularly true during the war, when bombings and black-out discouraged evening outings. News bulletins took on particular importance, but in addition regular programmes such as ITMA, Band Waggon, Monday Night at Eight and Garrison Theatre were weekly spots to which everyone looked forward. My only regret at this time was that my parents disapproved of advertising and refused to tune into Radio Luxembourg. To be the only girl in my form who was not familiar with the Ovaltinies was as bad as being excluded from a secret society.

I may not even have realised that the catchy song *was* an advertisement. The only things that I recognised as advertising were the ubiquitous cinema posters, and what they provided was necessary information. I must have seen the metal wall plaques bearing such brand names as Bovril, but it didn't register with me that knowing the name of a product was supposed to make me buy it.

There was very little pressure on children to be in the swim. Although from time to time a certain toy would become fashionable by word of mouth, it was easier to save up for a Yo-Yo than for a Game Boy or a pair of Doc Martens. There were no pictures of families with higher standards to excite envy and -- except for that Ovaltiney song -- no repeated jingles to make a child who lacked something feel out of the swim. Not in terms of ordinary life, at least. It was certainly true that the cinema pictured a way of life that made ours seem drab; but its glossiness was accepted as a fantasy world -- or, at least, something which only existed in America.

I soon came to take wireless for granted and enjoyed using my imagination to create scenery and fit faces to voices. The cinema was more exciting. My first experience of the medium was a frightening one. Florrie, the pregnant girl to whom my mother gave a few months' shelter, was so star-struck that she claimed -- and even appeared to believe -- that the father of her baby was Ronald Colman. In her short period as a mother's help she took me illicitly to the Harrow Coliseum, defying both my mother's rules and the age limits laid down by the film censors. A suspense film, totally unsuitable for a child and called, I think, The Clock Strikes Twelve, induced such nightmares that the expeditions were discovered and came to an abrupt end.

More appropriate to my age, a few years later on, were the children's matinees provided on Saturday mornings by a fleapit cinema on Harrow Hill. They were always so crowded that fighting for a seat was part of the excitement. Success in the scramble allowed the enjoyment of a serial along the lines of The Perils of Pauline, a couple of cartoons, and a film, probably already old, of the Will Hay or Jack Hulbert variety.

When the war began, films provided the most regular form of outside entertainment. My mother refused to go to the cinema on the grounds that she was not prepared to risk being killed in such surroundings: she seemed to feel that the company would be unsuitable to share her death with. My father, who did not sympathise with this view, took me along with him whenever he was at home between lectures.

There was a buzz about film-going. Queues were long, so that you could never be sure of getting in, creating a feeling of satisfaction as you reached the ticket office. Since the programme was continuous, members of the audience might leave at any time, so it was worth standing through a complete three-hour showing in the hope of getting a seat -- and if that meant sitting down in the middle of a film, well, there would be a chance to see the beginning later, and to stay through to the end again.

The Everest of cinema queueing was represented by Gone With The Wind, which showed no sign of ever emerging from Leicester Square. My father very reasonably jibbed at the thought of devoting a total of ten hours to such a venture, so a schoolfriend and I arrived two hours before the first four-hour performance of the day, in time to secure a safe position for the second showing. It was an opportunity not just for entertainment but for boasting as well.

Inside our local Dominion -- after an organist had risen grandly and loudly from below ground to entertain us before disappearing again -- the films were seen through a grey haze of cigarette smoke. The programme was a long one, because there would be a cartoon, a news, trailers and a B film as well as the title we had come to see: all but the cartoon probably in black and white. More important than anything else, the screen brought our heroes and heroines, larger than life, in front of our eyes.

Although at that time there were plenty of singers -- not only Vera Lynn -- who appeared and recorded with the big bands and who doubtless had their followings, the Forties equivalent of today's pop stars were the film stars. Even my mother was not immune, confessing to a weakness for Spencer Tracy. Because I found music more exciting than anything else, my own passion was for a singer: Nelson Eddy. While recognising that he was a wooden actor, I forgave him everything for the sound of his voice and kept a publicity photograph of him, impossibly blond, hidden at the bottom of a drawer. Both for a mother and for a novelist it's useful to have to have that kind of slightly shaming memory in one's past in order to empathise with today's screaming schoolchildren and to recognise that probably no one can escape a few years of fan adoration and fantasy.

The cinema became a once-a-weekly part of ordinary life: but the theatre was a treat: a marvellous experience. My father was an enthusiastic theatre-goer and I might have hoped to be taken regularly into the West End; but the war put paid to that. There was just time for me to enjoy a star-studded production which I can still recall almost word for word and gesture for gesture: The Importance of Being Earnest. The sight of John Gielgud's black top hat solemnly progressing behind a hedge as he prepared to announce the death of Ernest is not only the first but the most vivid of my best theatrical memories.

Another memory explains why such early recollections are few. Once again we were in the West End; this time at a musical. The sirens wailed an air raid warning. The show stopped in order that the audience could be told of the raid and given the choice of leaving for shelter at once or staying put until the all clear went. This was early in the bombing, and we stayed on. The show resumed; and after it was over the cast continued to entertain us with singing and dancing until they must have been exhausted. The audience was invited to join in the singing. As far as I was concerned it was a marvellous party, and I was sorry when the booming of anti-aircraft guns at last died away and the sustained high note of the sirens proclaimed the All Clear. But it was hardly surprising that there should have been no more expeditions of this kind.

So I was left to explore more local entertainment on my own. The Harrow Coliseum, changing from a cinema to a theatre, played host twice a year to the Carl Rosa touring opera company. Short fat tenors, necessarily well over military age, proclaimed their adoration of heroines so bulky that it was hard to believe that they were dying of consumption. Although I went as often as I could, it was not the best of introductions to opera.

Further away, but reachable by bicycle, was the Golders Green Hippodrome. This was a proper theatre, filled by touring productions. My memories are mainly of musical comedies -- Bruce Carfax in The Chocolate Soldier, or Richard Tauber, sadly past his best, as an unlikely romantic hero in Land of Smiles and Lilac Time. Most of the productions that I saw there during my teenage years were second-rate: but I recognised this and so they did me no harm. One evening with John Gielgud and Jack Hawkins and Edith Evans and the rest of a starry cast had shown me what good acting was, and the contrast provided by Golders Green served to reinforce my taste.

Just as I longed for deep hot baths after the war ended, so I longed for good theatre. To have been given a glimpse of it and then to find it no longer available left me desperate to catch up as soon as the bombing came to an end. As an undergraduate in Oxford there were two theatres to choose from, the New and the Playhouse, offering an adventurous diet which included early performances of Britten operas and verse dramas by Auden and Isherwood. When, many years later, we came to live in Oxford it was a disappointment to find that one theatre seemed mainly content to offer one-night stands to pop groups and that the Playhouse was on the point of closing, to remain dark for four years: it was a special pleasure that Jeremy should have been asked to chair the campaign which was successful in reopening it.

Those of the London theatres which had not been bombed reopened before the end of the war, but it was not easy to get a seat. During my underfunded time as an undergraduate I spent a good many vacation weeks working as a shop assistant and after a day on my feet the sight of a 'Standing Room Only' notice made me groan. But I paid my money anyway, and Ralph Richardson and Laurence Olivier at the New Theatre were able to make me forget my aching legs. Some theatres helpfully allowed a small folding stool to be reserved for sixpence early in the morning, to keep a place in the gallery queue. The reward was a crushingly few inches of narrow bench, high above the stage. One of the later delights of increasing prosperity -- and one of the benefits of living in London -- was the ability to go to the theatre regularly, often on the spur of the moment, and to sit in greater comfort.

My later experiments in the dramatic field were probably influenced by this youthful excitement in theatre-going. But it was a stimulus which came only from the outside, and successful writing has to come from within. There were different influences, nearer to home, which determined the field in which I was eventually to work.

Pen or platform

The books which provided my staple reading diet came free for the most part: as gifts, from the public library, or from my father's own collection. There was no limit on my access to them, but they were not enough to feed my voracious appetite. Magazines provided additional snacks; although magazines cost money.

My parents, predictably, took a low view of comics. Words, not pictures, were the stuff of education. *The Children's Newspaper* and Arthur Mee's *Children's Encyclopaedia*, which arrived in the house in regular parts, were heavy going for a young child, coming perilously near to homework. I did find the encyclopaedia, although not the newspaper, full of fascinating facts; but when I grew older and was allowed to make my own choices, adventure and fantasy took over at once.

If there were weekly magazines for girls -- and there must have been -- I had no time for them. *Hotspur* was my favourite reading, with *Magnet* introducing me to the excitements of boarding school life, as seen by the pupils of Greyfriars. Incomprehensible concepts like Shell and Remove merely added a touch of mystery to the promise of non-stop adventure and I longed to become a boarder myself.

There was, as it happened, a hook on which to hang this hope. It must have been the period of the 'guinea pig' experiment in which public schools were prepared to accept an occasional child from a state school, and at the age of twelve I became aware that Wycombe Abbey offered a free place to a girl nominated by Middlesex County Council. I indicated to my form mistress that I would like to enter, when the right time came, for what I saw as a competition.

She received the news with some surprise, being probably more accustomed to receiving such an approach from parents, and pointed out that there were several thousand girls of my age in the county, and I was not the cleverest twelve-year-old even in my own school. But although I was not yet carrying around a written version of my inelegant motto, its message was already in my mind. *Somebody's got to: why not me?* It didn't occur to me at the time that even a free place would undoubtedly have lumbered my parents with impossible expenses in the way of uniform and travel. No doubt the school warned them of my curious ambition so that they could talk me out of

it when the time came: but when the time did come -- for entry at thirteen --
the war had started, Wycombe Abbey had had its buildings commandeered,
and there were other things to think about.

Long before I became a parent myself, my views on the subject of
boarding had changed. The best environment for any child, I argued, was
surely a happy home with access to a variety of cultural experiences --
books, music, art, sport. Day school, in other words. Marriage to someone
who was equally convinced of the virtues of a public school education
brought the need for compromise. Before any baby actually joined the
family, Jeremy and I agreed that I could keep any girls at home and he could
send any boys away -- but not before the age of twelve. The idea of packing
a seven-year-old off to prep. school seemed barbaric to me at the time. Now,
as I watch Dragon School boys happily dashing round their playing fields, I
suspect that I may have been wrong. Too late.

Since we conveniently had one girl and one boy, it was easy to put the
concordat into effect. But my own twelve-year-old longings were not
forgotten. It seemed only fair to ask Jocelyn whether she would like to go to
boarding school, and I did so -- though the fact that she claims to have no
memory of the proffered choice suggests that I may not have pressed the
delights of the system too hard. It certainly made me happy that she chose to
stay at home.

I grew out of boarding school magazines just as I grrew out of
boarding school longings, and soon *Hotspur* and *Magnet* were replaced as
my favourites by such snippety magazines as *Titbits* and *Answers*. But these
provided only entertainment. It was a journal with a very much smaller
circulation which was to prove important in my life.

When I was about twelve years old my father gave me, as a Christmas
present, a year's subscription to a magazine called *The Children's Digest*.
This proclaimed itself proudly, if not very snappily, as being 'the only
magazine written and edited by children for children'. A friend of his had set
it up as a hobby occupation for his daughter, Carol Mary Spero, who was
three or four years older than myself.

The contents of the first issue were not particularly interesting, with
the exception of one short paragraph which announced that contributions to
the magazine (from children) would be welcomed -- and payment would be
made for those printed!

Every Monday morning at school we had to write something called a
composition: we all presumed that this was to allow our teachers time to

deal with the registers without having to teach. Variety was encouraged, so that my exercise book contained poems and stories as well as the usual 'favourite book' and 'holiday activity' subjects. It didn't take me long to find three poems and make my first journalistic submission.

All three were accepted; although since only one would be printed at a time and the magazine came out every two months I should have a long wait before I could hope for another success. Never mind: when the first poem appeared in print I received a complimentary copy of *The Children's Digest* and a postal order for half a crown. This may be only the equivalent of twelve and a half pence now, but in 1938 it was more than my pocket money for a month: my professional career had started!

Over the next two years I had a contribution printed in every number. After those first three offerings I wrote the items specially, including a serial story. I had learned the first rule of the writer: study your market.

This was to prove good practice for the time when, immediately after my marriage, I applied to become editor of an almost equally obscure children's magazine -- a post for which I had no visible qualifications. It quickly emerged in the course of the interview that I would be expected to provide most of the contents as well as edit them. 'Do you think you could write a serial story?' I was asked; and was able to reply with confidence that I had done that once already. But that lay in the future. At the time, the pleasure of seeing my own words in print was almost sufficient reward, although I did recognise that neither my output nor the magazine itself ranked very high in the literary world.

Another satisfaction was that of earning money by something more congenial than gardening or mending my father's punctures. My ambition to be a singer, already shaken by the realisation that I lacked the necessary talent, began to fade. Why should I not earn my living one day as a writer?

There were two answers to this question: equally unsettling. My father by now was producing books at a steady rate: he *was* a writer. But he was a cautious man who needed the security of a steady income, and was at great pains to point out that authorship was a precarious occupation which could easily lead to destitution.

My mother's attitude was almost the opposite. She would have liked to be married to a poet who cared nothing for money. Perhaps in his courting days my father had fitted this description, but whenever -- only half in joke -- she raised the subject, he was quick to point out that poetry would not buy butter. More privately to me she described the disadvantages of being married to an author: the periods of silence and withdrawal when he was broody with some new idea, and the frequency of his disappearances to the study to work when he should have been taking part in some family activity.

All this I dutifully observed. It took me a little while to realise that although there might be disadvantages in being the wife of an author, if I were to be the author myself, it would be my husband who suffered.

Writing this many years later, I know that the perfect solution for my mother's problem has been for one author to be married to another, so that there is mutual respect for the need for silence and solitude. And the equally perfect solution to my father's dilemma is for a novelist like myself to be married to someone who not only writes in his free time but also earns a salary and is willing to adopt the role of patron. Although this is how things have happened to turn out, rather than being the result of any plan, I have been luckier than either of my parents.

My mother did on one occasion attempt to solve her resentment at being cut off by the closing of the study door: she wrote a novel herself. It was called *In the Mouth of the Wolf* and its composition was preceded by many months in which beautiful phrases were shaped and written on cards, ready to be incorporated into the work at some suitable point: not an approach which lends itself to good story-telling. When the immensely long book was finished she sent it to one publisher, who rejected it. This affected her almost as though one of her babies had been murdered and she never submitted it anywhere again.

I found this decision impossible to understand -- to do all that work and then simply put it in a drawer! My disinclination to do almost anything at all in the way my mother would have done it was to serve me well later on. When my own time came for submitting novels to unenthusiastic publishers, I remembered what had seemed to me a feeble acceptance of defeat and refused to take No for an answer. For six years I sent off first one manuscript, then (to separate publishers) two and finally three, at monthly intervals (since in those days publishers took only three weeks to write their rejection letters, instead of three months or more.) The postman, ringing the bell to return them at regular intervals, became a sympathetic friend. The first book of mine to be published, *Murder to Music*, had been rejected fourteen times before it eventually found a home and proved what I have always believed: that determination is just as important as talent.

The typescript of *In the Mouth of the Wolf* lay in a cardboard box at the back of my garage for twenty years before dampness destroyed it. To allow any created work to disappear, even accidentally, is a cause for shame, and I *am* ashamed. If I were asked without having time to consider an answer, I would claim that I have no true addictions or blocks; but I would be wrong. I could never bring myself to read more than the first chapter of my mother's novel.

All those rejections lay far in the future while I was submitting my contributions to *The Children's Digest*. For the moment I was a Published Author; and before long there was more glory to come. Some members of the school staff became upset by an article, written by a master at a boys' school, which had appeared in the *Times Educational Supplement*, rubbishing the scheme which sent schoolchildren to work on the land. I was as indignant as my teachers, and without being asked wrote a long article describing a day at Temple Grafton and all the various achievements of our own school camp. To my delight it was published -- and the fee came not in half crowns but in guineas (which in a fit of altruism I spent on a suitable picture of a harvest scene to present to the school). This was a proper, grown-up market and marked a turning point. Words, not music, would be the tools of my career -- and they would be my own words, instead of somebody else's music.

In the meantime, another form of writing had proved attractive. An odd event in the annual timetable of Harrow County School was the Geography Prize. This was not, like other subject prizes, won by an essay. Instead, each form below the sixth form was allocated a country and required to write, produce and perform a ten-minute play about it. 3B found itself landed with Denmark: a rather flat subject. Through the eyes of Hans Christian Anderson I assembled a cast of fairy-story characters and caused some amusement by the manner in which they were required to digress from the plot to spout statistics on butter or bacon. For an eleven-year-old it was not a bad effort: not bad at all. 3B won the junior prize: and we continued to win as we progressed up the school. My best friend Joan Murray was a gifted actress: I always wrote and produced the play and she was always the star.

These small successes led to other opportunities, including the far more ambitious production of a pageant for the League of Nations Union, of which I was an enthusiastic member. I did for a time envisage a career as a playwright and, indeed, later wrote half a dozen plays which I hoped might be suitable for television. A drawerful of rejected scripts speaks of hours of work which were stimulating but ultimately a waste of time. The market was small and I lacked the right contacts. In this field it did seem that determination might not be enough by itself. It needed to be augmented by theatrical experience; and that was a snag.

Although I never performed in the little plays I wrote myself at school, I did a considerable amount of acting in the upper school drama group. While my friend Joan was usually cast as the heroine, I was a big girl and -- except for one moment of glory as Shaw's St. Joan -- found myself type-cast as heavy male. Heavy in the sense of important as well as overweight: from Bob Acres, I progressed to Shylock and on the strength of that performance was given the part of L'Avare -- The Miser.

This was a tough role for a sixteen-year-old girl, for the part had to be learned and spoken in French. I had an acute attack of stage fright. It didn't prevent me from going on: but as I raved and ranted, rolling about the stage in a long woollen dressing gown and an unconvincing cotton wool beard, I came to the firm conclusion that I was not cut out to be a performer. In my own modest phrase, as I turned down the opportunity to crown my school career with a King Lear, I had decided that I would rather be Shakespeare than Shylock.

Well, perhaps not Shakespeare, since rightly or wrongly I had already begun to realise that only someone connected with the stage was likely to write good plays. What I had in mind was to be a mixture of Dickens, Jane Austen, Graham Greene and Upton Sinclair. Especially Upton Sinclair. That copy of *The Jungle* which I had read at far too young an age had left an indelible impression. Long before my eighteenth birthday I had settled on my vocation: I was going to write Novels of Social Significance!

Ah well! Not every ambition can be fulfilled. I did try. I had -- and still have -- a burning belief in the right of the individual to end his own life if he chooses. My earliest attempts at novels invariably included a scene where, for example, one character, on entering a room in which another character was gassing himself, automatically opened the window but then thought for a minute and closed it again. Since attempted suicide was at that time a criminal offence, this storyline did not find much favour with publishers.

Yet there is a tenuous consequence of this idealistic ambition. I have never enrolled myself under any feminist banner, but there are one or two points which lend themselves to being emphasised in novels: not stridently but repeatedly, in the hope that they may become part of a changing climate of opinion.

The films which I saw in the Thirties and Forties preached the message that the most appalling behaviour could be justified by the defence of being in love, and that marriage was the only goal in life of any normal girl. I feel sure that this insidious gospel influenced the behaviour of many impressionable adolescents. It's to be hoped that perhaps a few girls in later generations may equally have been influenced if over and over again, in books of all genres, they have found themselves reading about a different kind of heroine: a woman who doesn't consider marriage until she is old enough to have established herself as an independent personality, who asks herself what she can contribute to society and takes any training necessary to make herself useful -- and who, if she does decide to marry, regards this as a beginning and not an ending.

I wouldn't find it easy to point to one of my own books and claim, 'This is important': but I hope that an Anne Melville heroine is a certain kind of woman who has helped in the nebulous process of persuading other women -- real women -- that there is nothing freakish about pausing to consider before handing their lives over to someone else.

None of that could possibly have been in my mind when I sent off my first poems to *The Children's Digest*, but there is a link: gossamer-fine, perhaps, no stronger than the thread of a spider's web, but leading straight from that thin yellow magazine to the fat volumes of 'family saga' which chronicle the adventures of the Lorimers or the Hardies, in which all the strongest characters are females. Once I had begun to write for a market, it was not too far-fetched an idea -- even in my early teens -- that I might one day create not just occasional verses but whole novels. After all, there was an example in my own home to demonstrate that writing books was even more satisfying than reading them: my father, the author.

Bernard Newman

For an example of the linkage between cause and effect I need look no further than my father's life and death. In 1918 the explosion of a German gas shell embedded splinters of metal in his mouth and throat. Most of them were removed; but apparently not all. A sliver which still remained caused a tumour to grow in the roof of his mouth. The growth was slow, but eventually, as he grew older, required a series of operations to remove it, and an ever-larger false roof. From the last of these operations he never recovered consciousness. He was over seventy by then; but his death was, nevertheless, the consequence of an injury sustained in battle more than fifty years earlier. Died of wounds.

The same theory could be operated in a negative way; the 'what if..?' argument. Bernard Newman was born in 1897, and as a consequence was condemned to suffer two world wars as an adult. He volunteered for the army while still under age and spent so long fighting in the trenches and then awaiting demobilisation that he was anxious to marry and settle down to earning a living as soon as he returned to civilian life. For this reason he never took up the Dixie exhibition which he had been awarded before he left Bosworth School.

Had his birthday been a mere five years later, his whole life would have been different. He would certainly have gone to Cambridge. He might still have become a civil servant, but as a graduate would have been eligible to enter a higher grade. Instead of merely using his undoubted administrative abilities, he could have hoped, as he became more senior, to influence policy in the course of his work instead of seeking another means of alerting public opinion to the international crises which he very early saw approaching. This in turn might have reconciled him to remaining in the civil service, with all the financial security it offered.

From such a scenario he would have emerged as a different man: less worried about money and possibly also less ambitious to be successful in a career pursued out of office hours -- and therefore slightly less disappointed when it did not achieve quite the level of respect which he felt it deserved. The pleasure he took in wearing the thin red ribbon of the Légion d'Honneur made me realise how much he would have appreciated some recognition from his own country of all the hours he had devoted to explaining international affairs to the public.

Although he never spoke of it at all, I had always understood how deeply the traumas of his life in the trenches had affected him. But it was only after his death that I was really able to comprehend how urgently he must have felt the need, after the loss of his youth in the wasted years, to catch up and to achieve fame and fortune.

A single incident opened my eyes to that, but first came all the sadness of losing a loved parent. His death sealed off my childhood in an unexpectedly abrupt manner. My mother had died in 1966 and in the same year he married for a second time. He warned me apologetically just before the marriage that he would have to change his will in order to provide for his much younger new wife, who would be losing her divorce settlement on remarriage.

The financial aspect did not upset me: I have never wanted to be one of those people who wait greedily for inheritances, and I hoped that his new marriage would bring him more happiness than he had enjoyed in the final years of the old one.

Nor, when the time came, did I feel any sentimental regret about the sale of the house: more than twenty years had passed since I ceased to live at 3 Gerard Road, and for several teenage years before that I had longed to escape from it. What *did* startle me, though, was the discovery that all the contents of the house in which I had been brought up were now my stepmother's property.

There was no good reason why this should cause distress. There was nothing of great value there, and I was living comfortably in a house which contained everything I needed. But it *was* a shock, all the same. Probably no will is ever probated without causing someone's feelings to be hurt. My sister Hilary had already -- far too young -- died of a brain tumour; but Laurie was upset when she was expected to pay for the piano which had been promised to her -- but not in writing -- years earlier. I was equally hurt to be told only at the last moment that all the books in the house were about to be removed by a bookseller: books which were not only a poignant souvenir of my father, but also an important part of my own growing-up.

I had time to retrieve just a few, and then it seemed sensible to close my mind to the disappearance or appropriation of what were, after all, only objects. My childhood was long gone: let it go. But the decision to make a clean break with such memories was attacked by two polite requests from my stepmother.

There was a problem about death duties. The size of my father's estate had come as a surprise not only to me but to the official who was dealing with the duty on it. If his income tax returns had been correct, it would seem that he had managed to save almost everything he had earned in the past twenty years, so obviously, it was argued, the figures could not be correct. My stepmother had not known the household for long enough to provide an explanation. She had to rely on me, and with a heavy heart I painted a picture which was true but not kind.

After the second world war -- in which he worked as a lecturer for the Ministry of Information -- he had decided to leave the civil service and live on what he could earn by writing and lecturing. Abandoning not only a regular salary but also the prospect of a pension was a big step to take, and he was never afterwards completely free of anxiety about money.

It was a fact that after his three children -- all educated in the state system -- had left home he spent practically nothing. A small inheritance of my mother's had paid off the mortgage on the house. He didn't drink, he didn't smoke, he had never owned a car and he had no wish to eat fancy food in restaurants. He travelled all over Britain to lecture, but his fares, meals and overnight accommodation were always provided by the societies who booked him. He flew all over the world to collect material for political and travel books, but he invariably persuaded some airline to give him a free ticket in exchange for a few flattering words in the resulting book. During my mother's long illness she was cared for by occasional visits from a National Health Service GP and the affectionate daily help of an undemanding Irishwoman. His own operations, at the Middlesex Hospital, were also on the NHS. There were never any private medical bills to pay.

My explanation -- which didn't entirely succeed in convincing the relevant authorities -- was true, but I hated writing it. It seemed to paint a picture of a mean man: not the man I knew at all. But before long a second request was on its way to me, and this was the one which opened my eyes.

By now the house had been sold and my stepmother had moved into a small flat. Would I, she asked, help her to sort out my father's papers, since she had no room to keep them all? I felt some resentment at this request. If he had appointed me his literary executor, I would have done everything possible to keep his reputation alive. But he hadn't, and I had neither rights nor duties. All the same, out of politeness, I went.

What I was shown came as a shock. The albums of press cuttings were not too much of a surprise. No doubt a good many authors like to collect their reviews, and I had known that for many years he subscribed to a press cuttings agency. Nor was it unusual that he should have kept letters from a variety of famous authors to whom, clearly, he had sent a copy of a novel in the hope of eliciting a favourable and quotable comment. The shock was that he had kept *everything*, however trivial. 'Dear Mr Newman, I confirm that I will meet you off the 6.58 on the 14th, as agreed on the telephone.' As I began to look through the files which covered more than forty years it seemed clear to me that all this had been filed for some future biographer.

Naturally I had known for many years that Bernard Newman had eventually achieved success as a very popular lecturer and author: this was the first moment in which I discovered just how ambitious he had been at the start of his career. The sheer volume of what he produced in his spare time during the first twelve years of my life would have been enough in itself to make clear his determination to succeed; but here were copies of all the letters he had written in his efforts to make his name known. Long before I had carefully encoded my own personal motto, he had been prompted by the same hopefulness, even if it was not expressed in so many words. Somebody's got to become a published author. Somebody's got to be one of the literary successes of the nineteen-thirties. Why not me?

If this came as a surprise to me, it was because of the contrast with what I saw of him at home as a child. He took unaffected pleasure in being a celebrity in the ambience of the Baptist Church and was even more proud, on visits to Ibstock, of being the village boy who had made good in London. But outside these familiar circles he was shy, even gauche, in face-to-face social contact. It hardly seemed possible that the same man could have written such forceful, pushing letters as he pressed his claims on publishers and editors in the early days.

From the moment he arrived in London after the Great War he set to work to establish a literary career. He wrote short stories and articles for magazines, plays for amateur dramatic societies and humorous songs and monologues for the concert party he had formed with a friend. It was in 1926 that he completed his first book. The arrival of a new baby -- myself -- meant that my mother could not travel with him that year: he set off alone to explore Andorra, at that time almost unknown in England. The book he wrote about his journey -- the first of many travel books to come -- sold only 700 copies and made him no money, but it was the start he needed.

For a time after that he experimented with novels of different kinds.

The Cavalry Went Through was a war book, realistic in every detail except that its hero managed to win the war in 1917. *Armoured Doves* was an early example of science fiction: the rays which penetrated armour plating and forced the world to live in peace were more magical then than they might be now. *Hosanna!* was a 'what if..?' book: what if Jesus had agreed to become the leader of a Jewish rising? *Death of a Harlot*, daring for its time, had prostitution as its subject. *Death in the Valley* was a fictional version of the origins of the Oberammergau passion play. He might have continued to experiment in this way for a long time, interspersing such differing novels with travel books, had it not been for the book which was published in 1935.

Spy was an immediate success. Bernard Newman was its chief character as well as its author; and Victor Gollancz, the publisher, amused himself in advertisements by encouraging doubts as to whether the book was fact or fiction. I sometimes think that my father himself was infected by the publicity -- it came as a surprise to me when I started to learn German at school that, far from being bi-lingual, he was not even able to help me with my elementary homework. In fact, when -- after the second world war -- we were able for the first time to go abroad together, I quickly realised that he was no linguist at all. Both my children have inherited their grandfather's delight in lonely travelling, but they must have acquired their skill in languages from some other source.

From the the moment when *Spy* was published his work as an author and lecturer was far more important to him than his civil service career, in which he could see little chance of promotion. His travel books -- researched with the help of his bicycle, George -- became increasingly interesting; and more important still were such political studies as *Danger Spots of Europe*, a subject which also proved a popular lecture. But the success of *Spy* brought a penalty with which every author is familiar. When one book does well, the publisher demands more of the same and the temptation to continue on a winning streak is very great. My father's total of 140 published books includes 54 novels: but after *Spy* there was a certain sameness about them.

So prolific was his output at one period that he was producing more books each year than librarians were prepared to buy from a single author. His solution was to use a pseudonym for some of his detective stories, and so Don Betteridge was born. I made use of the Betteridge name myself later on. When, after years of rejection slips, I eventually had two manuscripts accepted in the same joyful week, I was asked by the publishers concerned to use two different names to indicate that the stories were of different kinds; my father took great pleasure in learning that he was the progenitor of both Margaret Newman and Anne Betteridge.

Bernard Newman was a popular novelist in every sense, and no doubt he came to settle for that, but I feel sure that to begin with his sights were set higher. He would have liked to become one of the literary giants of the decade, but it didn't happen.

A child, of course, takes her father as she sees him. I was rightly proud that my father was an author and took for granted the absences and silences which this entailed. At home he was an easy-going, unassuming man who, like most breadwinners of his time, took it for granted that his wife would provide all necessary domestic comforts. With the exception of that single slippering, his involvement in family discipline was confined to an occasional mild 'Do as your mother tells you.'

He was not a kissing and hugging man. Once we had outgrown the stage of being jogged on his knee he rarely touched his daughters. I, for one, preferred this to my mother's regular demands for shows of affection, and have inherited enough of his reserve to feel uneasy about the general social kissing which seems to be required nowadays. Like many people who find it difficult to demonstrate love for human beings, he tended to overdo his enthusiasm for pets: from Tiddles, the black cat of my childhood, to Binker, the over-indulged Yorkshire terrier who provided company for his later years.

Both his salaried work and his outside career provided occasional perks. At the Office of Works he supervised the royal parks and, like some lord of the manor, was ceremonially presented with a haunch of venison once a year. More dramatically, he was involved in the arrangements for both the Silver Jubilee of George V and the Coronation of George VI, and I was able to watch both processions from the steps of grandstands in The Mall.

The private work introduced one or two unusual elements into the house. His early lectures were illustrated, with the help of a Magic Lantern, by heavy glass slides which he carried around in stout wooden boxes. He acquired one or two sets of slides suitable for children -- fairy stories and wild animals -- which I was allowed to colour from bottles of special ink: I became a lecturer myself, to an audience of my two sisters.

He wrote his books very fast in longhand, and his handwriting was even more illegible than mine is now -- an almost straight line with occasional wobbles up or down. Eventually he did manage to find just one typist who could decipher his writing, though he always found it worrying to put the only copy of a manuscript in the post to her. The ceremony of wrapping the parcel to be registered was one in which I was allowed to help. There were no sticky parcel tapes to secure the brown paper, so that when the string had been carefully knotted a stick of red sealing wax was heated with a match and held until a blob had fallen on each knot. While the search for that perfect typist was still going on, however, he experimented for a time with a Dictaphone, which recorded his voice on a turning drum of black wax. This was a popular machine with all his daughters, since we could record concerts with which to entertain our parents.

Not exactly unusual, but not to be taken for granted in the Thirties, was the telephone, which we acquired earlier than most families I knew in order that my father could arrange his lectures and concert party performances. At first all calls went through an operator, but eventually we were converted to automatic dialling. The first three units to be dialled were expressed in letters, taken from the start of a word to make them stay in the mind. To remember Wordsworth 2468 from fifty years on is much easier -- for someone who is more literate than numerate -- than to recall a modern number consisting of a long string of figures. But although the telephone was invaluable to my father, it was not much use to me, since none of my friends' parents were subscribers and it takes two to make a conversation.

All these were insignificant possessions, but they contributed to the ethos of a household in which writing was not merely something to be taken for granted, but the only thing worth doing. How could such an atmosphere fail to have an effect? Quite easily, it might seem, since neither of my sisters showed any inclination to become writers. But then, they were never able to enjoy, as I was, the six years of being an only child; and their wartime evacuation removed them from the household for a long period. I alone was exposed to my father's influence for the whole of my youth. And although he was a kind and affectionate father to all three of us, I never doubted for a moment that I was his favourite.

By his way of life he showed me that to be a novelist is a perfectly normal activity; but there must be another kind of cause and effect to explain why my path has in many ways followed his: something in the genes, perhaps. Like my father, I started with ambitions to be a 'good' writer, whatever that may be; but like him again I discovered that in fact I was 'only' a popular writer; a story-teller. Like him, in the field of fiction, I have found myself trapped by the 'more-of-the-same' preferences of publishers, and two separate editors have frustrated my attempts to extricate myself from their ruts.

My inheritance is more positive even than this. From the moment he resigned from the civil service, my father never stopped writing. He wrote not only all day in his study but in trains, in planes and in hotels. It was not merely a way of earning a living but an addiction which needed its daily fix. I suffer -- if it is suffering -- in the same way, although not to the same degree. I have more hobbies and a happier home life and, thanks to Jeremy's support, have no actual need to write a single word for money. None of that can quite banish the feeling that a day in which I have written nothing is a day wasted out of my life. After posting off a new manuscript I may promise myself a week's holiday, but within two days can bear the idleness no longer: it's time to start on the next book.

It is perhaps because I recognise this obsessive need to write as an addiction that I am not afflicted by the disappointment which my father felt about the limitations of his literary reputation. I note with a certain amusement that if I write a particular genre of book -- a crime novel, or a children's book -- it will be favourably reviewed, whereas a much better book for the 'women's library market' will not be reviewed at all, but it doesn't worry me. I am delighted by the high Public Lending Right figures which tell me how many thousands of readers borrow my books, but that is only a comparatively recent comfort. The act of writing fiction is enough in itself to make me happy: the most pleasurable occupation that I can imagine.

So this link is the clearest of all in the game of consequences. I came into the world as the daughter of Bernard Newman, author. The result is that I became an author myself.

First love

Does this section, I wonder, truly qualify for inclusion under the title of Consequences? A first love affair is an important part of anyone's growing up; and mine, extending over several years, brought me a good deal of happiness and some grief. But as I begin to write about it, I'm unable to think of any effects which can be said to have flowed from it. It was a thing-on-its own; an interlude.

There was not much scope for romantic love in an all-girls day school. Even the crushes which schoolgirls develop for glamorous members of staff were not much in evidence at Harrow County, where the teachers were conscientious but, with one exception, physically unattractive and lacking in charisma.

The exception was the senior games mistress, whose boyish figure looked far better in a gym slip than did most of her pupils and whose profile, her devotees thought, was that of a Greek god. My lack of enthusiasm for gymnastics and lacrosse, and my exclusion from tennis coaching, meant that I never liked her, but I was in a minority.

In my last year at school, as school captain, I became a favourite of the headmistress, who once or twice invited me to dinner at her house and almost always rostered me for firewatching on the same night as herself. It was while firewatching that I was given a short talk on an alternative version of the facts of life. This shed some light on a book which I had earlier borrowed from my father's top shelf. Radcliffe Hall's *The Well of Loneliness* had been printed in Paris and covered in plain brown paper after being set, presumably, by a printer who spoke no English. Its thousands of misprints made the simple act of reading hard going, but in addition I had completely failed to understand what the book was about.

A little light now penetrated this bemusement, but I was given no time then to think about it. Would I please, asked the headmistress, study my fellow-members of the Upper Sixth carefully and report to her if I discovered any unhealthily close friendships?

I had no intention of sneaking about what seemed to be none of my business, or hers. But with my eyes thus opened, it didn't take long for me to notice that a girl who wore her hair boyishly cropped and preferred to be called by a boy's name was often to be found cuddling another member of the Sixth. And now that I was on the alert, I developed a second suspicion: that the headmistress herself and the games mistress were a great deal friendlier than they ought to be. It was all very interesting.

I had friendships with girls, but I didn't love them. As for boys, they hardly figured at all for the first sixteen years of my life. I did have three boy cousins, and in the attic bedroom which we shared during their visits I was able to note with surprise various differences of anatomy. Brian was ten years younger than myself: almost a different generation. Graham, my own age, suffered from rickets and wore irons on his legs, but did not attract my sympathy. Only Keith, three years older and clever, became a friend. We did experiments from our chemistry sets together and spent hours setting out and playing the complicated game of Tri-Tactics; but the cousinly relationship was never a flirtatious one.

School provided no boy-friends. Except for an occasional marble-shooting competition, I had no wish to play with the roughies of Greenhill Elementary, and certainly spent no time with them outside the playground. Harrow County, of course, was single-sex. Black-out and air raids combined for long periods of the war to discourage dances or other evening gatherings for schoolchildren: parents worried, and children accepted it as reasonable that they should stay at home and get on with their homework. The only parties to which I was invited were birthday celebrations, held in the afternoon and for girls only.

Towards the end of the war a dance was arranged for the Harrow County Girls' and Boys' Schools combined. This caused a flutter in the sixth form, and wet dinner hours were devoted to the laborious learning of ballroom dancing steps -- slow, slow, quick-quick, slow -- to the accompaniment of Victor Sylvester records. But the dance, when it came, was not a success. Both boys and girls, who did not know each other, were reluctant to approach strangers. Girls danced with other girls: boys did not dance at all.

There was, however, the Baptist Church. Just as it provided games of tennis and dramatic rehearsals, so too it offered opportunities for matchmaking. My mother could think of nothing better than that I should grow up to marry the son of one of her Baptist friends. She even chose the lucky boy for me. Worse than that, she told us both what she had in mind. Since Grant was only twelve at the time and I was eleven, the prospect of one day settling down together was inconceivable and highly embarrassing. Until then we had quite liked each other as we moved up Sunday School together, but as soon as we gathered what was envisaged the friendship shattered. He pulled my long hair; I stole his best pencil, and was glad when his family moved to Glasgow.

As I grew older, I didn't miss what I had never had; the company of young males. But at the age of sixteen -- what an earnest young woman I must have been! -- I spent a week of the Easter holiday in Cheltenham, at a conference organised by the Council for Education in World Citizenship. One of the other attenders was a seventeen-year-old from Bolton, who was just about to take -- and win -- a scholarship to read philosophy at Cambridge. He was the first boy -- youth -- I had ever met who was not just clever but an intellectual. I was not exactly swept off my feet: all I wanted during that first week was the pleasure of talking to someone so much brighter than myself. But I certainly accepted with enthusiasm the suggestion that we should correspond, and I can remember feeling almost faint with excitement when the first long letter arrived.

Correspondence -- even after subsequent meetings brought first kisses, first declarations of love -- proved to be the backbone of the relationship. To begin with, I was in Harrow and Donald was in Bolton. I remained at school while he joined the Navy. I went up to university and he was part of the occupying force in Germany. When at last he was able to take up his scholarship, it was not at my university. Our meetings, during leaves and vacations, were brief, hobbled by the fact that we were both, as undergraduates, chronically hard up.

Nevertheless, the relationship blossomed. It would be more precise, I suppose, to call it a romance rather than a love affair, because nothing actually happened. Unplanned pregnancies were very much feared both by men who might be trapped into marriage and by girls who would see their studies and careers lost, quite apart from their reputations; and contraceptive advice was not at all easy to come by: my own GP, when agreeing several years later to help, required me to confirm in writing that my wedding date was set for not more than a month ahead. But in our case I don't think that such a fear was a major factor. We had both been brought up in Christian families, and took it for granted that pre-marital, like extra-marital sex was Wrong.

My own upbringing, indeed, was stricter even than that, since it was my mother's belief that a girl should not kiss a man unless she had already decided that she wanted to marry him. Even as an inexperienced sixteen-year-old I thought that was carrying things a bit far, but some of her attitude must have rubbed off on me. Certainly I believed that I ought only to be on kissing terms with one chap at a time, and felt very strongly that no girl should ever allow a man to get to the point of proposing marriage unless she intended to accept. The memoirs of such 1920s flirts as Barbara Cartland disgusted me by her pleasure in collecting and rejecting dozens of proposals.

It was taken for granted by most girls of my age that marriage -- eventually -- was what we wanted. Because, in the 1930s, teachers who married were forced to give up their jobs, we were all being taught at school by women who were the lonely victims of the Great War carnage: not enough young men had survived to provide husbands for them all. We were sorry for the spinsters, but determined not to meet the same fate ourselves. I can think of none of my schoolfriends who deliberately planned to devote herself to a career. My own intention was not just to work but to continue working after marriage; but even this was a relatively new idea. As I discovered when the time came, no female either in Jeremy's family or in my own had ever done so before.

So, when marriage was proposed to me, I accepted joyfully, while realising that it would have to be a distant prospect. The engagement, however, did not last long. Alarmed by the commitment, Donald suggested that it should be replaced by an 'understanding' and, confident in our feelings for each other, I agreed. A year later the pattern was repeated: engagement on, engagement off. This time I was upset, and decided that I ought to behave more positively instead of merely reacting. There were going to be no more on-off episodes. I was not going to marry Donald. I was not even going to consider the possibility any longer, since it had begun to spoil our friendship rather than enhance it.

From this decision flowed a marvellous sense of freedom. During my first terms at university I had avoided any kind of emotional entanglements, considering myself, whether by engagement or understanding, to be committed. But now there was nothing to stop me from developing new friendships: and this was just at the time, after the war, when ex-servicemen were flooding back to start or resume their studies: mature young men in their twenties, very different from the unfit eighteen-year-olds who had been allowed to take up their university places in wartime. The ratio of men to women undergraduates rocketed. I stopped being an over-serious one-man-girl and began to enjoy myself. It was then that Jeremy entered my life.

I was still corresponding with Donald, and we were both honest in our letters. It didn't take him long to realise that I was falling in love again. He turned up in my college room unexpectedly one afternoon. I don't know what he hoped, and I doubt whether he knew either; the visit did nothing except to make it clear that the 'off' switch was permanently down.

There were no serious quarrels, and no great obstacles in the way of this first love: except one, and it was large enough. We had met too soon. War service added an unwanted extension to the length of time which a future professor would need to acquire a first and then a higher degree before he could think about settling down to marriage.

If Donald was afraid of committing himself to what would have been an extremely long engagement, I sympathised completely. If he believed that it would be unfair to commit me to such a wait, he was in fact mistaken. I enjoyed the emotional security of knowing that I was loved, but had no wish for an early marriage. My ideal prospect was of an engagement during which I could go and work abroad, knowing all the time that someone would be waiting for me to return -- and, in fact, this was precisely what Jeremy gave me, since he too needed time to complete his degree and find work.

All these later developments took place after my eighteenth birthday; but it was before that time that a pattern was established which did after all, as I realise now that I have set it down, have later consequences. What I have described was a relationship which, from necessity, was to a great extent developed by correspondence. It gave me pleasure to write long and frequent letters, and even more pleasure to receive replies. This must have been true for a great many people in wartime; but I never lost the habit.

When I was abroad I wrote home to Jeremy. Back in England, I wrote first to my sister and later to my daughter and son as they each in turn worked overseas. This covered a period of more than twenty years, and I felt quite deprived when they were all living in England again. I don't think it's a coincidence that the only one of my school friends with whom I have kept in touch has lived in the United States for the past forty years. We only meet once a decade, so letters are the main link. And my friendship with Donald, still continuing, is maintained more by letters than by visits.

This must say something about my attitude to friendship. I have never had close friends of the 'drop in for a cup of tea' kind. Friendship by correspondence is no doubt selfish, allowing the writer to choose the time which she will devote to any one person, as well as the topics to be discussed. But for someone who can marshal her thoughts on paper better than in conversation, it is satisfying; my pleasure in it dates from the month after I returned from a conference in Cheltenham, at the age of sixteen.

Going for gold

I can't remember exactly when I first decided that I wanted to study at Oxford. I had no acquaintance with it as a place, although on the evidence of the photograph album I was taken on a day trip at the age of four. My first true introduction to the university came through Helen Waddell.

I was about thirteen when I read *Peter Abelard* -- thirteen and young for my age. In spite of my precocious study of *Enduring Passion* I read the novel without having the slightest idea what exactly was the nature of the punishment meted out to the unfortunate Abelard -- just as at much the same time I devoured all the volumes of *The Forsyte Saga* without ever knowing what Soames had done to Irene that was so wicked.

At that age, if I enjoyed a book, I hurried to read everything else by the same author, and so one day I carried home from the library a copy of *The Wandering Scholars*. By the time I finished it a door had opened into the future. I wanted to be part of this tradition of scholarship. It was not so much a new idea stirring my interest for the first time as a simple certainty that this was where I belonged. My sincerity can be judged from the fact that gratitude to Helen Waddell even carried me through her volume of *Medieval Latin Lyrics*, although Latin was far from being my favourite subject.

At the age of sixteen I announced that I wanted to go to Oxford. In the novels and autobiographies that I read, young men decided to go to Oxford and so they went. It didn't take long to discover that for a young woman it was not quite as easy as that.

The difficulties emerged gradually. First to be recognised was the sheer competitiveness of the situation. Application had to be made to a college, not to the university, and no college would have more than four or five places to offer in any particular subject. The odds against winning one of them were long indeed.

As if that were not daunting enough, my father threw a financial spanner into my hopes. He certainly wanted me to enjoy the university education that he himself had missed -- but what he had in mind was London University. I would be entitled to a county grant to cover my fees and could continue to live at home, travelling up each day and costing no more to support than when I was at school. Sending me to Oxford, with maintenance to be paid, would be far more expensive.

There was nothing wrong with London University and several of my schoolfriends were heading there. But I was stubborn in my choice and at last my father agreed to a compromise. I could go to Oxford if, and only if, I won a scholarship.

I accepted what he said about the financial implications and it didn't even occur to me that he might merely be testing my resolve. I can't have had the faintest idea of the task I was setting myself in accepting the condition. There were four women's colleges and one society of home students at Oxford: a maximum of five scholarships a year in each subject to be tossed into the pool of clever girls all over England.

And now I discovered yet another difficulty. Harrow County School regularly fed its sixth-formers into London University on the strength of their Higher Certificate results; but it had little experience of preparing them for the very different Oxford scholarship examination. According to the honours board, one girl had won a scholarship six years earlier. It was not a very cheering statistic.

To crown it all, I had a small spanner of my own to throw. I had always been good at English, regularly coming top in exams and winning poetry and essay prizes. But an unexpected flash of insight suggested to me that learning Anglo-Saxon and dissecting Chaucer and Shakespeare was as likely to spoil my pleasure in both reading and writing as to enhance it. I decided to read history instead, and therefore to sit for the scholarship in that subject.

This was a mistake from which a more sophisticated school could have saved me. I was simply not aware that there were subjects other than school ones which could be studied at university. When I finally arrived at Oxford and discovered the existence of PPE -- Philosophy, Politics and Economics -- I felt some disappointment that nobody had told me about it before:, because it was just what I would have liked; but by then it would have cost me too much to change.

In other respects the school did its best for me. I had delivered a blow to my English teacher, Miss Leeds, who might have hoped that I would bring her honour. But a member of the staff who was herself an Oxford graduate coached me in the writing of the 'general essay', dealing out subjects from past papers and criticising my efforts every Saturday morning. In addition, a weekly history tutorial was arranged, to be shared with a girl from North London Collegiate School who was preparing for the same examination. This, although useful, did little for my morale, for Gitta was beautiful, sophisticated and clever: one of the five scholarships was disappearing before my eyes.

Because of the war, there could be no question of staying on at school for a term after taking Higher Certificate, which was the usual system in peacetime. I had to enter for the examination in my fourth term after Matriculation, at the age of seventeen. However, I was to be allowed two bites at the cherry. Somerville, the college on which I had set my sights, had its entrance examination in March: but in November I could have a trial run by taking the joint examination for St Hugh's and St Hilda's. I knew nothing about either of them, but it would be good practice.

November approached at a rush, for the autumn term of 1943 was a busy one. The Oxford preparation was additional to regular work for Higher Certificate and I had also now been elected School Captain, responsible for timetabling and supervising all the prefects' duties. There was harvest camp again in September and fire-fighting vigils once a fortnight. At one moment everything was hectic and then suddenly quietness descended and time stood still. I followed the invigilating member of staff up to an attic room in the sixth-form house and a notice was placed at the bottom of the stairs. Silence please: examination in progress.

Scholarships and ordinary places were all to be awarded on the strength of a single examination. The colleges had announced in advance that only borderline cases would be called for interview. When my summons came from St Hugh's College there was nothing to indicate whether I was on the edge of failure or of success.

For the benefit of candidates with long journeys, there was the offer of a night's accommodation in Oxford. I could easily have made the return journey inside a day, but had no intention of turning down the chance of more time to explore. I arrived in the city on a dark, rainy December night.

The odd thing, I realise now, is that nothing seemed odd at the time. I came up to an Oxford which was a figment of my imagination and found exactly what I was looking for -- the medieval home of the wandering scholars.

Consider the special circumstances of wartime. St Hugh's College itself had been taken over as a military hospital for the treatment of head injuries so I was to stay at Holywell Manor, which still retained traces of its sixteenth century origins. I set out from there for a walk. Every window was blacked out and I was not aware of any modern buildings as I wandered down Longwall Street, into the High, up Queen's Lane, over the cobbles of

Radcliffe Square -- all free of traffic in a time of petrol rationing. Stone and silence. Illuminated by slits of light from shielded street lamps, the rain fell in solid diagonal lines in front of the black stone walls of New College Lane. This was the wet, marshy Oxford to which the wandering scholars had come: it was just what I had expected.

Early next morning I walked along the towpath from Folly Bridge. A mist was rising from the river; the same mist which greeted and sometimes killed those medieval scholars -- for Oxford was notorious for its miasmas and fevers. I sat there for a long time, until it was time to attend a twentieth-century inquisition in a seventeenth-century Holywell house.

I was greeted as 'Miss Newman'. Nobody had ever addressed me in that manner before: I stepped straight from childhood into adult life.

In other respects, however, the interview did not start well. Poking the inadequate fire as though the movement might supply more warmth than the single lump of coal could, Miss Proctor, the history tutor, remarked that she had rarely been confronted with a scholarship candidate whose translation from Latin bore so small a resemblance to the original. In 1943 both Latin and a foreign language were compulsory subjects. Alarmed, I tried to defend myself. Virgil had certainly given me trouble, but I was under the impression that my rendering of one of Cicero's orations had been a spirited effort. I had understood the point he was trying to make; but had apparently been carried away by my own eloquence instead of his, scribbling down what he might well have said, but didn't. It had sounded rather good, I thought at the time.

A very little of this I tried to express, and the conversation took a curious turn. Instead of discussing the Tudors and Stuarts we talked about relationships between fact and fiction, historical record and propaganda, and then about the sound of language as opposed to its content. I was in a Swinburne phase at the time and quoted with enthusiasm lines which sounded glorious but meant very little. In almost her only direct question of the interview Miss Proctor stabbed again at the fire and asked me whether I wrote poetry myself. It was clear that no good could come of a truthful answer. I sighed as I gave it. 'Yes. Well, verse.'

Had she pressed on, it would not have taken her long to realise that I was applying for a history scholarship mainly in order not to spoil my love of literature; but fortunately at that point one of the long silences for which she was famous fell upon her. I took the opportunity to see what could be retrieved from what seemed to be a disaster and plunged into an account of what I knew of Oxford's history -- and the feelings it had inspired in me. It was the romantic, sentimental stuff of a seventeen-year-old's imagination -- and to a real historian must have seemed as fictional as my rendering of Cicero -- but it was sincere. Miss Proctor thanked me politely for coming: I would hear from the college before Christmas.

I must in fact have posed a problem for her. St Hugh's was not a rich college. Not more than one scholarship was offered in any subject each year and, thanks to our respective places in the alphabet, a proper history scholar had already presented herself for interview before it was my turn to climb the Holywell stairs. Olive Gee, who later became a friend, was easily recognisable as someone who would go on to get a First and enjoy a respected academic career. I was not, and Miss Proctor had almost certainly realised before I did myself that my talent was to be for fiction. But something in the interview must have struck a chord. In the year of my admission there were, exceptionally, to be two scholars to read history at St Hugh's.

The night of my mastoid operation provided the first vivid memory of my youth. The afternoon of December 22nd, 1943, supplies the final one.

It was the last full day of the school term, although on the next morning there would be a special assembly followed by a general tidying up and emptying of desks and lockers. My mother was ill, so instead of staying at school for lunch I cycled home to prepare a meal for her. A second post had been delivered in the course of the morning and there was a letter for me. The Principal of St Hugh's College, Oxford, had much pleasure in telling me that the College had elected me to a major scholarship in Modern History.

I ought to have felt an enormous relief, for certainly the waiting period had been an extremely anxious time. But what I remember is more an intense satisfaction. Now that it had actually happened, the award of the scholarship seemed so exactly right that it was almost impossible to believe that it could have turned out any other way. 'Somebody's got to', my ugly motto reminded me; and the missing word was 'win'.

I took soup up to my mother and gave her the news before flying back to school on my bicycle. The rest of the day passed as a personal triumph. It was the afternoon of the annual carol concert, attended by parents and governors. I was a member of the orchestra which played a squeaky overture as the school filed in. I was school captain, and made my way on to the platform to welcome the governors. Instead of returning to the orchestra I moved to the senior choir, to sing a solo part. And at the end of the afternoon the headmistress -- pleased not only for my sake but because she was telling the assembled mothers what the school could do -- announced the winning of the scholarship.

This success did not solve all problems. The scholarship provided more honour than cash, and my years at Oxford were penurious. Nowadays a good many students are hard put to it to make ends meet, but in 1944 a high proportion of my fellow-undergraduates came from public schools and had wealthy and generous parents: I took the difference to heart as I spent vacations as a shop assistant or washer-up. It was necessary to remind myself that those medieval scholars had been poor as well: I was still following the tradition.

This poverty had a small consequence of its own. Although at the time I accepted the fact that my father could not afford to fund me more lavishly in case my mother should need expensive care later on, I was startled after his death to learn how much my stepmother was inheriting. It made me determined to give as much as I could afford to my own children when they needed it and while I was still alive, instead of keeping them waiting for an inheritance, and I was glad to find that Jeremy shared that attitude.

More seriously, my examination success led me for a time down a false trail. To be a scholar carried weight in the college. I wore a special gown and took different examinations from the commoners. I was encouraged to work in Duke Humfrey's library as well as in the Radcliffe Camera. The constant emphasis on my status led me to believe that I was in fact a scholar, in the general sense of the word. For at least a year and a half of my undergraduate life I ignored many of the special benefits which Oxford has to offer in order to swot -- and even envisaged an academic career for myself. This would have been a mistake, and it was fortunate that instinct led me to the writing of fiction.

What might have been equally dangerous was the reinforcement of an existing belief that I -- and anyone else -- could achieve any goal merely by wanting it enough. It seemed to me then that determination was always more important than talent. Now, when I recognise disappointment in other people, I have to accept that this cannot possibly be true and that I might have laid myself open to great disappointment of my own. However, the theory of all-conquering determination was later to carry me through dark periods when all my babies miscarried and all my novels were continually rejected; so it has worked for me. I have always been lucky in the end.

Although the winning of the Oxford scholarship felt at the time like a single step along the straight path which I had mapped out for myself, it was in fact a turning point, with consequences that I could not have foreseen. Social consequences, intellectual consequences, but, most important of all, the consequence of happiness. Had I not gone to Oxford I should never have met Jeremy and never have had children -- or, if I had, they would not have been Jocelyn and Jonathan. More than forty years of happy married life have resulted, indirectly, from an interview which took place when I was seventeen.

*   *   *

Miss Proctor, the history tutor, later became Principal of St Hugh's College. Many years afterwards Jeremy and I met her by chance in Portugal. The encounter reminded me of the confession that she had extracted from me in her Holywell room and -- just as I once turned my notes on Gilbert Ryle's lectures into rhyme -- I spent the evening scribbling, with this result.

Ballade
On meeting the Principal of an Oxford college
in the streets of a Portuguese village.

Sixteen summers and springs ago,
Silvered and shyly collegiate,
You warmed the room with an evening glow,
Stirring the fire in an Oxford grate.
You fed my desire to re-create
The truth of history's right and wrong
And, lost in the past, to meditate,
'This is the time of my golden song.'

Fourteen summers and springs ago,
Suddenly claiming youth's estate,
I weighed the past, and I let it flow
Out of my mind, insatiate
With love and with life, and desperate
To grasp at the time-devouring throng
Of moment on moment; to jubilate,
'This is the time of my golden song.'

Taking the evening paseo,
I meet you today with your scholar's gait
And, suddenly young again, I know --
Fourteen summers and springs too late --
Joy journeys with us; it does not wait.
The heart has its youth, which travels along
The path of our age immaculate:
This is the time of my golden song.

Envoi

Principal, old and expatriate
Here is the moment where we belong.
The past is a lonely and barren state.
This is the time of my golden song.

Even by the standards of occasional verse this does not rate high, but I enjoyed writing it and it includes a couple of lines which I still secretly cherish. I realise now, though, that it contains one important mis-statement. There is nothing barren about the past. It contains the seeds of all our harvests.

Excuse

When I was fifty-eight years old I discovered that I had breast cancer. I had for some years been carrying out the regular self-examination which is recommended to women, and one Thursday night I went through the routine as usual. Nothing there. Good.

At eleven o'clock the next morning I was sitting at the word processor with all my attention concentrated on the novel I was writing, when my body interrupted my mind to tell me in unmistakable terms that I ought to do the examination again. So clear was this instruction that I reached for one of the reference books I keep in the study -- a textbook of medical-surgical nursing, invaluable whenever one of my characters is condemned to ill-health. When I looked up breast cancer, I discovered a page of illustrations which I had never noticed before: a step-by-step guide to self-examination. It was immediately clear to me that what I had been doing in the past was useless. I moved into a bedroom, propped up the illustrations, started to prod and found the lump almost at once. A visit to the doctor next day merely confirmed what I already knew.

The discovery did not greatly alarm me. It would be tough on Jeremy if the condition proved serious, but at least Jocelyn and Jonathan were adult and independent: the great anxiety of any mother is that she may die while her children are still very young, as my sister Hilary had done; and I had passed that stage. I had had a good life and I have never wanted to grow very old. There was nothing to cry about.

There was, however, a question to be asked. Suppose, I said to myself; suppose I have only another year or perhaps two to live. Is the novel which I am writing at this moment the one to which I would want to devote those last precious months? This, of course, is the question that every writer should put to herself about every book. I was ashamed to realise that the answer in this case was No.

Second question: then how would the time be better spent? This time the answer took me completely by surprise, as I discovered that I wanted to write about my childhood. I set to work the same day. although the success of an operation a week or two later led me afterwards to enjoy the marshalling of memories at a gentler pace.

The urge to write autobiography is an odd one. Famous people, or those who have survived exceptional circumstances, may expect readers to be interested in the events of their lives. Great stylists may hope to give pleasure simply by the beauty of their writing. But someone like myself, with an ordinary life and an ordinary literary style, has no such justification: only an unexpected wish to organise the confused threads of early life into some kind of pattern.

It's as well to recognise that the whole exercise is self-centred and self-indulgent. I may have tried to persuade myself, as I delved into memory for the contents of sweetshops or the words of Sunday School hymns, that my daughter and son would be interested in a picture of their mother's early years. But the truth is much simpler than that. I am a writer, and to a writer nothing is quite real until it has been written down. I am real. I have existed. These are the words which prove it.

And the consequences were...

By *Margaret Newman*

Murder to Music

By *Anne Betteridge*

The Foreign Girl
The Young Widow
Spring in Morocco
The Long Dance of Love
The Younger Sister
Return to Delphi
Single to New York
The Chains of Love
The Truth Game
A Portuguese Affair
A Little Bit of Luck
Shooting Star
Love in a Rainy Country
Sirocco
The Girl Outside
Journey from a Foreign Land
The Sacrifice
A Time of their Lives
The Stranger on the Beach
The Temp
A Place for Everyone
The Tiger and the Goat

By *Margaret Potter*
(for children)

The Touch-and-Go Year
The Blow-and-Grow Year
Sandy's Safari
The Story of the Stolen Necklace
The Motorway Mob
Tony's Special Place
Trouble on Sunday
The Boys Who Disappeared
Tilly and the Princess

(for adults)

Unto the Fourth Generation
Lochandar

By *Anne Melville*

The Lorimer Line
The Lorimer Legacy
Lorimers at War
Lorimers in Love
The Last of the Lorimers
Lorimer Loyalties
The House of Hardie
Grace Hardie
The Hardie Inheritance
The Dangerfield Diaries
Snapshots
The Tantivy Trust
A Clean Break